QR Codes
FOR
DUMMIES®
PORTABLE EDITION

D1617368

by Joe Waters

Co-Author of *Cause Marketing For Dummies*

WILEY

John Wiley & Sons, Inc.

QR Codes For Dummies®, Portable Edition

Published by
John Wiley & Sons, Inc.
111 River Street
Hoboken, NJ 07030-5774

www.wiley.com

For general information on our other products and services, please contact our Customer Care Department within the U.S. at 877-762-2974, outside the U.S. at 317-572-3993, or fax 317-572-4002.

For technical support, please visit www.wiley.com/techsupport.

Wiley publishes in a variety of print and electronic formats and by print-on-demand. Some material included with standard print versions of this book may not be included in e-books or in print-on-demand. If this book refers to media such as a CD or DVD that is not included in the version you purchased, you may download this material at http://booksupport.wiley.com. For more information about Wiley products, visit www.wiley.com.

Library of Congress Control Number is available from the publisher.

ISBN 978-1-118-33703-5 (pbk); ISBN 978-1-118-36211-2 (ebk); ISBN 978-1-118-37071-1 (ebk); ISBN 978-1-118-37291-3 (ebk)

Manufactured in the United States of America

10 9 8 7 6 5 4 3 2 1

WILEY

About the Author

Joe Waters has been working at the intersection of business, philanthropy, and marketing for nearly 20 years.

Joe writes the web's leading cause marketing blog, `http://www.selfishgiving.com`, which chronicles his insights on building successful nonprofit and for-profit partnerships.

He is a sought after commentator on how nonprofits and businesses can use cause marketing, social media, and mobile technology to establish, grow, and deepen relationships with stakeholders.

Joe is the co-author of *Cause Marketing For Dummies* and a contributor to *The Huffington Post, The Chronicle of Philanthropy, Mediapost, Forbes,* and *The Nonprofit Quarterly.*

Joe lives with his wife and two children in Newton, Massachusetts. You can follow Joe on this blog at `http://selfishgiving.com` and on Twitter at `@joewaters`.

Dedication

To my children, Cate and Ryan, who are guiding my way through the real maze that QR Codes just look like.

Author's Acknowledgments

Few books are written and published by one person, this one included.

I owe a big thanks to my QR Code consigliore Noland Hoshino. In addition to serving as the technical editor of the book, he was an invaluable source of information and inspiration on QR Codes. I'm proud to call him a friend and colleague.

Chad Sievers guided the completion of the book with skill and compassion. Thank you, Chad.

Heidi Unger copy edited my manuscript with interest, humor, and care and helped produce a much better book.

This is my second tour of duty with Amy Fandrei, acquisition editor at John Wiley & Sons, Inc. It just gets better every time!

Of course, I would be remiss if I did not acknowledge the love, support, and sacrifice of my wife, Debbie.

Publisher's Acknowledgments

We're proud of this book; please send us your comments at http://dummies.custhelp.com. For other comments, please contact our Customer Care Department within the U.S. at 877-762-2974, outside the U.S. at 317-572-3993, or fax 317-572-4002.

Some of the people who helped bring this book to market include the following:

Acquisitions and Editorial

Project Editor: Chad R. Sievers

Acquisitions Editor: Amy Fandrei

Copy Editor: Heidi Unger

Technical Editor: Noland Hoshino

Editorial Manager: Jodi Jensen

Editorial Assistant: Leslie Saxman

Sr. Editorial Assistant: Cherie Case

Cover Photo: ©iStockphoto.com / SimplyCreativePhotography; ©iStockphoto.com / franckreporter; ©iStockphoto.com / Presiyan Panayotov

Cartoons: Rich Tennant (www.the5thwave.com)

Composition Services

Project Coordinator: Kristie Rees

Layout and Graphics: Carl Byers, Lavonne Roberts

Proofreader: Dwight Ramsey

Indexer: Potomac Indexing, LLC

Publishing and Editorial for Technology Dummies

  Richard Swadley, Vice President and Executive Group Publisher

  Andy Cummings, Vice President and Publisher

  Mary Bednarek, Executive Acquisitions Director

  Mary C. Corder, Editorial Director

Publishing for Consumer Dummies

  Kathleen Nebenhaus, Vice President and Executive Publisher

Composition Services

  Debbie Stailey, Director of Composition Services

Table of Contents

Introduction

*W*hen I first accepted the offer to write *QR Codes For Dummies,* my initial thought was, "How am I going to write a whole book on QR Codes?" They are the simplest of digital tools. Writing about QR Codes was like writing about a screwdriver, another simple tool (that as of yet doesn't have a *For Dummies* companion).

Sure, the numbers behind QR Codes are impressive. QRStuff. com, one of the world's leading websites for creating QR Codes, recently reported that 2.1 million users generated 2.7 million codes in 2011, an increase of 1,253 percent.

That's a lot of QR Codes, and all from just one generator!

Still, probably a hundred times that number of screwdrivers are in every country in the world. So popularity wasn't a good reason to write an entire book on QR Codes, or *Screwdrivers For Dummies* would've been a bestseller.

QR Codes are book-worthy because although screwdrivers are a tool for driving screws, a QR Code is highly versatile. They're a key that unlocks something greater than expected and are a portal between the real world and the digital world. You can't say that about a screwdriver.

QR Codes are simple tools that are powerful. They're kind of like the ring Frodo Baggins carries in the trilogy *The Lord of the Rings.* They may be small and simple, but the ring and QR Codes are big medicine.

About This Book

The good news is that the journey you and I are about to begin isn't like Frodo's. You don't have to worry about any danger, powerful wizards, or heavy burden to save the world. All that's required for this journey is curiosity.

You may be one of the millions of people who've already scanned a QR Code, but you're wondering, "How can I use QR Codes, and what possibilities do they hold?"

I aim to show you their potential, but I also encourage you to just play around with QR Codes and use this book less as a rule book and more as a guide. Like a QR Code, scan it for what you need and let your own ambitions and needs drive where the book takes you.

Foolish Assumptions

You don't need much to get started with QR Codes, but you do need a few things. I made the following assumptions when I wrote this book:

- ✔ QR Codes aren't much fun or very useful if you don't own or have access to a smartphone. You can skip ahead to Chapter 2 to determine if you have such a device for reading and creating QR Codes.

- ✔ The book requires a basic familiarity with the Internet. Although you can use QR Codes for a number of things (such as dialing a phone number, sending a text, accessing a map, and so on), most codes link to a URL. If you're not familiar with searching and using the Internet, you may want to start by familiarizing yourself with the online world on a desktop.

- ✔ QR Codes are like seeds. After they're planted, you must have faith that they'll grow. QR Code use is just beginning to take off, especially in the United States and Canada. Not everyone is convinced the QR Code seed will grow. But you the reader must have faith and patience and share Henry David Thoreau's belief that if you show me a seed, "I am prepared to expect miracles."

Conventions Used in This Book

Like every *For Dummies* book, I use the following conventions to help you.

> ✔ When I introduce a new term, I *italicize* the term and follow with a clear and concise definition.

> ✔ When I present a list of important terms or pointers, I **bold** the keywords that introduce each bullet.

> ✔ When I include URLs of websites, I don't break off long URLs with dashes or hyphens to help you when you type the URL into your browser.

> ✔ When you see a QR Code in the left margin, scan it with a reader (which you can read about in Chapter 2) to access additional content. I promise that scanning these QR codes will enhance your learning on QR Code use and marketing.

Icons Used in This Book

You'll see these little icons scattered throughout the book. These icons flag additional, helpful information.

Tips provide helpful information and advice I've picked up using QR Codes.

This icon means *Whoa!* Following my advice here might just keep you out of a lot of trouble.

Remember icons are just that, pieces of information I want to remind you of. Circle it, highlight it, fold over the corner of the page — but don't forget it!

This icon points to technical information that you may or may not want to read depending on your interest in the subject or technological savvy. Geeks love this stuff!

Where to Go from Here

Depending on your knowledge level, Chapters 1 and 2 are great places to start. Reading Chapter 1 can make you happy you bought the book. Reading Chapter 2 can get you scanning QR Codes if you haven't already.

From there, skip around the chapters as you like. Be sure to pause at the final chapter, which gives you ten practical uses for QR Codes, because you may find some uses for QR Codes you hadn't thought of.

Also, be sure to check out my Pinterest pin board of QR Codes. Noland Hoshino, the technical editor of the book, and I have been gathering good and bad examples. In the search box on Pinterest type in **QR Codes For Dummies** and then click on "Boards."

If you have any questions about what you've read, you can contact me via e-mail at my blog, www.selfishgiving.com. I'm also very active on Twitter. You can find me at http://twitter.com/joewaters. My username is @joewaters.

Speaking of Twitter, if you're interested in staying abreast of new developments in QR Codes, I have a suggestion for you that worked wonderfully for me as I wrote this book. Visit https://twitter.com/search and type **QR code** or the hashtag **#qrcode** in the search box. Twitter search operates much like Google search does for the web, but the former limits results to those found on the social networking site.

A great benefit of Twitter is that it delivers the best and latest information on just about any topic, including QR Codes. Because tweets are limited to 140 characters, they often contain links to longer articles, posts, videos, commentaries, and so on. I learned a lot more about QR Codes by just checking Twitter once a day for the latest tweets relating to QR Codes.

The key is to watch for tweets that are *retweeted* a lot, which means you see the same tweet reposted again and again by different people. This is a good indication that people find it useful, and you should click the link. There's a certain wisdom of crowds, you know.

Chapter 1

Understanding QR Codes

In This Chapter

▶ Defining QR Codes and explaining what they do

▶ Using QR Codes to connect the offline world with online content

▶ Understanding the value of QR Codes to your business

*Y*ou've probably seen more than your share of QR Codes. They seem to be popping up everywhere — magazines, direct mail, billboards, resumes, online, and even as tattoos on people's bodies.

I clearly remember the first time I saw a QR Code. Puzzled, I thought it looked like an aerial view of a cornfield maze created by farmers, or maybe even aliens! Fortunately, QR Codes aren't the work of farmers — or part of a sinister alien invasion — but their potential for organizations of all kinds is truly out of this world.

In this chapter, I explain what QR Codes are and how they're different from other types of barcodes. I also make the business case for QR Codes, show you who's using them — and who will be using them soon — and why they should be a permanent addition to your marketing toolbox.

Introducing QR Codes

Here's a trivia question for your next dinner party. What's the *QR* in *QR Code* stand for? Answer: Quick Response. QR Codes are a quick way to access information. That was the intent when they were first used in the auto industry to track parts. No more tracking long serial numbers — just scan and go. It's not surprising that businesses quickly saw the value of QR Codes on things other than fenders and bumpers.

Your basic QR Code, as shown in Figure 1-1, is a two-dimensional barcode comprised of small black squares within a larger square on a white background.

Figure 1-1: A QR Code.

You can access the information encoded on a QR Code with a smartphone equipped with a QR Code reader, as shown in Figure 1-2. The reader interprets the data on the code and redirects the phone's web browser to a destination predetermined by the code creator.

You can put a QR Code just about anywhere, including in these places:

- ✔ On a business card
- ✔ On a billboard
- ✔ In a book
- ✔ On a poster
- ✔ On a website
- ✔ On a carton
- ✔ On a sign
- ✔ On a wristband
- ✔ In an ad
- ✔ On top of a cake

Figure 1-2: Reading a QR Code by scanning it with a smartphone.

Where you can put a QR Code is limited only by your imagination.

In addition to appearing just about anywhere, a QR Code can accomplish a lot. You can do all these things — and more — with a QR Code:

- ✓ Open a web page.
- ✓ Begin a video.
- ✓ Make a payment.
- ✓ Play a song.
- ✓ Open a document.
- ✓ Like a Facebook page.
- ✓ Board a plane.
- ✓ Deliver a coupon.
- ✓ Download a smartphone app.
- ✓ Dial a phone number.
- ✓ Pass along a business card.

Here's an easy way to remember what a QR Code is: It's an *offline hyperlink*. Just as online hyperlinks, when clicked, can open every kind of content imaginable, QR Codes are their offline equivalent. They link content to more content.

Scan the QR Code in the left margin for a brief video introduction to QR Code technology from Scan.me.

Comparing QR Codes to Traditional Barcodes

QR Codes have been around since the 1990s, but traditional two-dimensional barcodes have been around for decades. It's safe to say that although the average consumer is becoming more aware of QR Codes, recognition of barcodes and what they're used for is probably close to 100 percent.

Barcodes and QR Codes both allow you to store information in a tiny space. If that's true, why not just use the more recognizable barcode instead of a QR Code? The answer is data: you can store more of it on a QR Code (see Figure 1-3). In a regular barcode you can encode data only vertically. In a QR code you can encode data both vertically and horizontally.

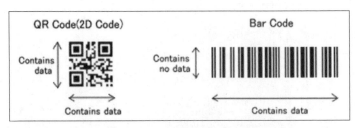

Figure 1-3: A QR Code allows you to store more information than a barcode.

QR Codes have these other advantages over barcodes:

- ✔ **QR Codes are readable from any direction.** If you've ever self-scanned your groceries at the supermarket, you know how picky traditional barcodes can be.

- ✔ **QR Codes are generally more durable.** The info in them can be decoded even if part of the QR Code is missing or damaged.

The jury is out on whether QR Codes will ultimately replace barcodes altogether. In a culture that prizes lots of information, data-rich QR Codes could easily be the barcode of the future.

Don't crown QR Codes the king of the barcodes just yet. In Chapter 9, I show you new alternatives to QR Codes that might just usurp their place on the barcode throne.

Bridging the Offline World with Online Content

The main value of QR Codes is that they quickly and easily link the offline world with online content. Until recently, offline and online content have been like the Earth and the Moon: two separate worlds. Offline, a business owner may have a sign outside her business with details on hours and specials. Online, she may have a website with the very same information.

However, a QR Code on a sign outside the store can bridge the two worlds (see Figure 1-4).

Figure 1-4: QR Codes can make ordinary store signs more engaging to patrons by linking them to interesting and relevant online content.

Duplicating information is one option, although I show you in Chapter 5 that's not the best use of QR Codes. Scanning a QR Code is at least as easy as, and more effective than, taking a picture for shoppers who want to "know and go."

A better way to use QR Codes is to have them to do some-thing the medium they're on, in this case a sign, can't do. For example, if the sign features daily specials, a QR Code can open a page of pictures of menu items to whet the customer's appetite. Or it could link to the restaurant's full menu or to the latest customer reviews.

The offline and online worlds are no longer separate. QR Codes are the bridge between the two.

Making the Business Case for QR Codes

You picked up this book, so you may already see the business value of QR Codes. I can quickly confirm that your assumption is right.

- ✔ **QR Code use is growing.** QR could easily stand for *quick rise.* According to Scanbuy, a leading mobile marketing company, in the third quarter of 2011, 44,000 Codes were generated — compare that to just 17,000 in the third quarter of 2010. The 44,000 codes accounted for more than 400,000 scans combined, an increase of 39 percent over 2010 results.

- ✔ **QR Codes deliver the information consumers want.** The Internet has created a whole layer of content that con-sumers consult before they buy or act on just about any-thing. Google has a good name for it: the Zero Moment of Truth (or ZMOT). More and more, this information is accessed via smartphones. QR Codes are an easy way for smartphone-toting shoppers to retrieve it.

- ✔ **QR Codes are made for the mobile consumer.** According to a Nielsen study in late 2011, more than 60 percent of 25- to 35-year-olds own smartphones. And among those 18–24 and 35–44 years old, smartphone owners hover near 54 percent. Even smartphone use among 55- to 64-year-olds is at 30 percent, up 5 percent in just one quarter. QR Codes are one of the best tools available to market to smartphone users, which someday soon will probably include just about everyone.

✔ **QR Codes are tiny, but powerful.** QR Codes can link to just about any kind of online content and display in just about any size. (See Figure 1-5 for an example of a billboard-sized QR Code.) But smaller will be the norm as QR Codes are more widely used and recognized. Shoppers are used to seeing barcodes on the tags of products they buy. Soon, they can expect to see QR Codes and be willing to search for them like most people search for barcodes in the self-checkout line at the supermarket.

Figure 1-5: QR Codes can be just about any size, but needn't be this big to be effective. Unless you like them this way.

Small is good for QR Codes, but not so small that they can't be scanned by a QR Code reader. Make sure your QR Code is at least one square inch with at least four millimeters of white space around it. See Chapter 3 for more guidelines.

✔ **QR Codes are versatile.** Most QR Code generators allow you to change the content they point to without changing the code itself. For example, if a QR Code near your register links customers to your monthly specials, the QR Code image can stay the same when the specials change. Just go online and change what it points to.

✔ **QR Codes are trackable.** Are you worried that your boss will question the value of this new technology and its return on investment? The good news is that you can track when and where your code was accessed, what type of phone was used, and the number of repeat visitors, among other things. Just like the Google Analytics you use to analyze the visits to your company website, analytics for QR Codes can keep tabs on visitors, analyze results, and help you adjust your marketing campaigns so they're more effective.

Looking at Who's Using QR Codes Today, Tomorrow

Research shows that men, ages 18 to 34, scan most QR Codes. They tend to be educated, and one-third make more than $100,000 a year. Men have been the primary audience downloading QR Codes since their inception in the early 1990s.

It shouldn't surprise you that men were the early adopters of QR Codes, nor should you assume they will always be the primary audience. If the history of other new technologies is a good teacher, the audience of QR Codes will shift to other key audiences over time.

Take the automobile, for instance. In 1900, more than 4,000 were built in the United States. At the time, the U. S. had a population of 76 million. Early car buyers and drivers were prosperous, educated men. Of course, that changed as the car became more commonplace in American culture. Today, both men and women buy cars.

More recently, young, educated men adopted technology such as Foursquare that allows them to share their location with friends and for nearby businesses to deliver location-based news, discounts, and specials. But that audience is shifting, too, and understanding why isn't difficult. Men might sometimes adopt products first, but women take it over because they do most of the shopping. According to The Boston Consulting Group, women control two-thirds, or 12 trillion dollars, of household spending.

Women are scanning QR Codes to unlock discounts, promotions, and giveaways. In a recent survey, 46 percent of respondents said they scanned a QR Code to get a discount. Women are driving these downloads and pushing businesses to create QR Codes that meet their needs.

Some businesses are already responding, according to *Adweek.* In 2011, women's magazines led the pack in QR Code use. *InStyle* was number one, with 141 codes that year. It was followed by *People* (136), *Self* (126), and *Entertainment Weekly* (123).

Beauty, home, and fashion brands are also using QR Codes in magazine advertising. In 2011, John Frieda used 82 codes; L'Oréal used 79; Cuisinart, 74; Garnier, 72; and Revlon, 67.

Men may be scanning more QR Codes than women, but if the history of automobile buying is any indication, it won't be long before women take their rightful place in the driver's seat.

Here's something that may quicken QR Code adoption among men and women and make them a household item: As QR Code use reaches a tipping point, the major mobile device makers (for example Apple and BlackBerry) may make QR readers — the app you currently need to download to read a QR Code — standard equipment on all their devices, as they already are on BlackBerry devices. Maybe even as part of the smartphone camera, as illustrated by technology journalist Wayne Sutton in Figure 1-6.

Figure 1-6: A native QR Code reader on smartphones would elevate QR Codes from curiosity to household name in a very short time.

Such a move would dramatically increase QR Code scanning. It would do for QR Codes what Google Maps has done for directions: made it a regular part of the mobile experience.

Stay tuned!

Something for everyone

QR Codes aren't just for the average consumer or for business-to-consumer companies. Companies that sell business to business can also use them. One innovative business, CRT Industrial Equipment, Inc., is using QR Codes to service customers who are spending up to $100,000 on just one piece of equipment. (See the following figure where the QR Code on the machine links you to a page where you can request a service or view online manuals. Scan it for yourself and see.)

Chapter 2

Reading a QR Code

• •

• •

*T*he first order of business is to get you scanning all the QR Codes that are popping up on billboards, signs, books, bumper stickers, key rings, and a million other places. If you're like me, you'll love scanning QR Codes.

Besides being fun and giving you access to all sorts of interesting and useful online content, people around you will point and whisper and ask why you're pointing your phone at a black and white maze. You should have a standard response, as I do. "I'm with the government, ma'am. Please stand back."

This chapter doesn't have any tips for using QR Codes to punk curious strangers, but I do show you how to pick a QR reader for your device. Many readers are available to choose from, both free and paid. I also show you how to scan a QR Code, what to do if it doesn't scan, and how to save the code for later use.

Picking a Reader for Your Phone

Some smartphones come with a QR Code reader installed on the device. Others require that you download one. A *QR Code reader* decodes the squares within a QR Code and redirects your phone to an online destination chosen by the code creator.

The most common first question I get is, "Can I read a QR Code with my phone?" It's an excellent first step. Or you may be hearing more jeers than cheers from bystanders who know you can't read a QR Code with an old flip phone. The following sections help you figure out if your phone is compatible and what readers are available.

Determining if you own a smartphone

Can you even scan a QR Code with your current phone? Do you own what's called a *smartphone,* as shown in Figure 2-1, or do you own the popular but quickly disappearing, feature phone? Here are a few tips to discover if your mobile device or phone is a "smart one" and can read a QR Code.

Figure 2-1: A smartphone looks and acts more like a small computer.

- ✔ **Is your phone a lot like a computer?** Smartphones tend to look and operate more like a minicomputer than a phone. If your device looks more like a phone, it's probably just that.

- ✔ **Can you access the web on your phone?** That's a great indicator that you own a smartphone and not a traditional feature phone. Because the main role of QR Codes is to link you to online content, you need web access for them to work.

✔ **Do you download apps on your phone?** This feature is common on smart devices, and you can download a QR Code reader if your device doesn't have one installed.

✔ **Does your phone have a camera?** You need a camera to be able to read QR Codes.

✔ **Does your device have a QWERTY keyboard?** This means the keys are laid out as they would be on a computer keyboard — and not numerically as they are on a feature phone. These keys are either physical (like those found on most BlackBerry devices) or on a touchscreen (like on Apple's iPhone).

If you're still not sure if your mobile device can read a QR Code with the right software installed, swing by the store at which you bought it and ask a representative to help you. If you don't own a mobile device that can read QR Codes, I'm sure they'll be happy to sell you one.

Choosing a QR Code reader for your operating system

The *operating system* on your smartphone is what runs it; it determines what QR Code reader you can use. Not all readers work on all phones, and assuming that they will is like assuming that a Ford muffler can fit on a Chevy exhaust system. It won't. Like every car, every operating system is different.

I distinguish QR Code readers by operating system in this section because the brand name on your phone (such as HTC, Samsung, or Motorola) may not help you choose the right reader. Knowing which operating system your phone uses will. Sound confusing? Don't sweat it. I show you which phones run which operating systems.

Determining your operating system is easier when you know that nearly 90 percent of all smartphones run on Android, Apple, or BlackBerry operating systems. Also, whatever device you own, you can't go wrong if you stick with the preloaded app store on your device. It's the direct link to QR Code readers — and other applications — that are sure to work on *your* device.

Choosing a reader for an Apple operating system

Finding a reader for your Apple device is easy for a couple reasons. First, all Apple devices come with Apple's operating system, so you don't have to worry that your Apple device is running a BlackBerry operating system (heaven forbid!). Second, Apple has an easy-to-use App Store at which you can download a reader.

Here's how to download a QR Code reader for your Apple device:

1. **Find and touch the App Store icon (see Figure 2-2) on your mobile device.**

Figure 2-2: Apple's App Store icon.

2. **Tap the Search button on the bottom right of the screen and type** QR Code reader **in the search field.**

   A list of QR Code and other barcode readers appears. Pick a free reader for now. I distinguish between free and paid readers shortly, but for the time being, here are the top three free readers in the App Store, based on customer reviews:

   • *QR Reader for iPhone* (4.5 out of 5 stars)

   • *Scan* (4.5 stars). This also works on Apple's iPod touch and iPad 2.

   • *Quick Scan* (4.5 stars). Also works on iPod touch.

   You can also search for these readers in the App Store by name.

3. **Tap the reader you want and tap FREE at the top right.**

4. **Punch in your Apple ID to download the app.**

Choosing a reader for an Android operating system

The Android operating system controls a whopping 40 percent of the smartphone market. It's no wonder that many popular smartphones, including those made by HTC, Motorola, Samsung, and others come with Android operating systems.

Some devices that run the Android operating system come with a barcode scanner. If yours doesn't, here's how to download a QR Code reader for your Android device:

1. **Find and touch the Google Play store icon (see Figure 2-3) on your mobile device.**

Figure 2-3: Android's Google Play store icon.

2. **Type** QR Code reader **into the Search bar.**

   A list of QR Code and other barcode readers appears. Pick a free reader for now. I distinguish between free and paid readers shortly. For the time being, here are the top three free readers in Android's Google Play store, based on customer reviews:

   • *QR Droid* (4.5 out of 5 stars)

   • *QuickMark Barcode Scanner* (4.5 stars)

   • *QR Barcode Scanner* (4.0 stars)

   You can also search for these readers by name.

3. **Tap the reader you want and tap** *Download* **at the top right.**

Choosing a reader for your BlackBerry operating system

BlackBerry devices run only BlackBerry operating systems. The good news is that some BlackBerry devices come with a loaded QR Code reader. The bad news is they don't call it a QR Code reader.

Here's how to locate it:

1. **Locate and press the Menu key on your device.**

2. **Select Scan a Barcode.**

If your device doesn't come with a built-in QR Code reader, or if you just want to try a different one, head over to the BlackBerry App World and download a third-party application.

1. **Find and tap the App World icon (see Figure 2-4) on your mobile device.**

Figure 2-4: The BlackBerry App World icon.

2. **Type** QR Code reader **into Search.**

A list of QR Code and other barcode readers appears. Pick a free reader for now. I distinguish between free and paid readers shortly. For the time being, here are the top two free readers in App World, based on customer reviews.

- *QR Code Scanner Pro* (4.5 out of 5 stars)

- *NeoReader QR Code Reader* (2.5 stars)

Are paid readers better than free ones?

To pay or not to pay for a QR reader? That is the question. Lots of free readers for Apple, Android, and BlackBerry devices are available, but you also find paid readers; most of them are just 99 cents.

But are they worth even a buck? The best thing about paying for a reader is that eliminates those pesky ads that come on most free readers. You may agree with me that it's 99 cents well spent!

Another benefit of paid readers is more features. A random search of readers revealed that paid ones touted these additional features:

✔ No ads.

✔ It reads all types of barcodes, including QR Codes.

✔ The app reads faster.

✔ The reader is also a QR Code creator.

✔ It includes the option to share QR Codes on social networks.

✔ You can see analytics on QR Code views and so on.

My advice is to carefully compare the features of your free reader to those of paid ones. You may be surprised that free readers have almost as many bells and whistles as paid ones. The biggest test for any reader is does it work and give you the results you want. If not, don't hesitate to try another free or paid reader.

The good news is that paid readers range in price from 99 cents to just a few dollars. If they do most of the things they promise, especially reading codes faster and delivering speedy results — and with no ads — your money may be well spent.

You can also search for these readers by name.

3. **Tap the reader you want and tap FREE at the top right.**

Scanning a QR Code: The Simple How-to

With a QR Code reader on your smartphone, you're ready to scan your first QR Code. Doing so is very easy. I walk you through how to use your QR Code reader by scanning the Code in Figure 2-5.

Figure 2-5: Scan this QR Code with your reader.

1. **Open the QR Code reader on your phone.**

   (*Note:* I'm using QR Reader for Apple's iPhone 4G. You may be using a different reader, but it will work in the same way.)

2. **Hold your device over a QR Code, as shown in Figure 2-6, so that it's clearly visible within your smartphone's screen.**

   Two things can happen when you correctly hold your smartphone over a QR Code.

   1. The phone automatically scans the code.

   2. On some readers, you have to press a button to snap a picture, not unlike the button on your smartphone camera.

3. **If necessary, press the button.**

   Presto! Your smartphone reads the code and navigates to the intended destination, which doesn't happen instantly. It may take a few seconds on most devices.

   If you correctly scanned the QR Code in the figure, you're now looking at my blog.

Figure 2-6: Position the QR Code within the screen of your reader.

This book walks the walk when it comes to QR Codes. I'm not just talking about them; I'm using them all over the place, and for the same reason you'll be using them: to educate, inform, explain, and for many other reasons that make QR Codes a great tool. Watch for them throughout the book and have your QR Code reader handy!

Troubleshooting QR Code Reader Failures

Sometimes your QR Code reader won't read the code, or the reader will just keep working like it's trying to do something but won't. Or it will take you to the wrong page or an error page.

I hate when that happens. You will too. Here are the first things I recommend checking:

✔ **Are you scanning a QR Code or a barcode?** I know it sounds silly, but I see people all the time trying to scan a regular barcode with a QR Code reader. The good news is that a lot of QR Code readers also read barcodes. But not all do, so this may be your problem. Don't forget what a QR Code looks like: small squares within a larger square on a white or light background.

✔ **Is your device connected to the Internet?** QR Codes link the offline world with online content, so being connected to the Internet is kind of important. If you're not on a network (such as AT&T, Verizon, Sprint, and so on) you need to be in a *hotspot,* a location with Wi-Fi. Even if you are, make sure you've enabled your Wi-Fi in your device's settings so it can find and connect with the network.

✔ **Are you too close to or too far away from the QR Code?** Most readers indicate a sweet spot, so to speak, within which your code can be scanned. Make sure the QR Code is within that area.

✔ **Is the QR Code blurry?** Make sure it appears clearly within the screen by moving your device back or forth to adjust the focus.

✔ **Is the problem the QR Code or your reader?** Try scanning a different QR Code. If your reader works, the problem probably lies with the QR Code.

✔ **Did the reader not scan a second code?** Try deleting the QR Code reader from your device and reinstalling it, or try a different reader. I give you several suggestions for QR Code readers for Apple, Android, and BlackBerry earlier in the chapter.

Saving a QR Code for Later Use

Whenever you view web pages, you record a history in the browser that you can refer to if you want to revisit the site later. Your QR Code reader also saves your scanning history. When you're out and about scanning QR Codes — perhaps standing in line at the supermarket checkout when you spot a QR Code on a register sign — you can capture them with your reader and view them later.

Just like your web browser, QR readers have a history option. You can review QR Codes at your leisure, so scan away.

If by chance your QR Code reader doesn't have a history page, the reader may allow you to scan a code right from your picture library. In that case, snap a picture of the code and scan it later.

Chapter 3

Creating a QR Code

· ·

· ·

*S*ome people are happy to spend their days scanning QR Codes and never think to create their own codes to use in their everyday lives. Others see these nifty, useful codes and ask, "How can I create and use my own QR Code?" This chapter is for the latter.

In this chapter, I help you choose a QR Code generator and show you how to make your own QR Code or find someone to do it for you. Next, I help you customize your QR Code with color or your logo for added appeal. Finally, I show you how to ready your QR Code and protect it from the untidy masses that will soon be touching, poking, and scanning it.

Choosing a QR Code Generator

You can easily find a QR Code generator online or in your device's app store. Many of the readers I recommend in Chapter 2 are also generators. The following sections outline some important features you want in a generator and explain the different ins and outs between online and mobile generators.

Eyeing important features

Regardless of whether you're creating a QR Code online or with a mobile app, consider these features when choosing a free or paid generator:

✔ **It creates a QR Code in a minute or less.** The goal is to have you use QR Codes in several different ways, but you can't if you can't create one on the fly. The generator you use, regardless of all the extra features it comes with, should allow you to create a QR Code in under a minute.

✔ **It produces a QR Code in a standard size.** Some generators, especially those found online, generate larger QR Codes when long URLs are inputted. But large, unwieldy QR Codes aren't practical or attractive. Stick with those generators that produce a standard-size QR Code with the option of making it smaller or bigger based on your needs, not on the size of your URL.

In general, use shortened URLs with your QR Code. Your QR Codes will be less dense, scan more quickly, and will be less likely to fail. Most generators can shorten URLs for you, or you can shorten them yourself at www. tinyurl.com, Goo.gl, www.bitly.com, and many other sites. Just type *shorten my URL* into your preferred search engine.

✔ **It gives you the flexibility to redirect the QR Code to a different destination whenever you want.** Some generators allow you to create a QR Code, but then you can't change what it links to unless you create another code. What a pain. Yours truly found this out the hard way when I included a QR Code in a brochure, and then a website redesign changed the URL that the code pointed to. Suddenly, I had a QR Code that went nowhere and I couldn't redirect it without reprinting the brochure. Avoid an awkward conversation with your boss and choose a generator that allows you to change the URL without changing the code itself.

✔ **It doesn't limit your QR Code campaigns to URLs.** Maybe you want a QR Code that dials a phone number, passes on contact information, opens an e-mail, or links to a map. Pick a generator that gives you the flexibility to choose what the code links to.

✔ **It gives you a way to track the QR Code.** I talk more about the types of information you can track with QR Codes in Chapter 6, but at a minimum, the generator should track the number of times the QR Code was scanned. This is a key data point in measuring the success of the code.

Picking the best online generator

If you type *QR Code generator* into your favorite search engine, you'll literally get hundreds of results. If QR Codes are a niche marketing tool, as some claim, you wouldn't know it from all the generators available. Here are my picks for the top three online QR Code generators.

Kaywa

Kaywa's QR Code generator (at http://qrcode.kaywa.com) is one of the easiest generators to use on the web (see Figure 3-1). Here's all you need to do to use it:

Figure 3-1: Kaywa's QR Code generator is quick and easy.

1. **Select the appropriate Content Type radio button.**

   You can choose from the following:
   - *URL*
   - *Text*
   - *Phone Number*
   - *SMS*

2. **Enter the content.**

3. **Choose the size of the QR Code.**
   - *S:* One square inch (perfect size for your business card!)
   - *M:* One and a half square inches.

- *L:* Two square inches.

- *XL:* Three square inches — a good size for a poster.

4. **Click Generate!**

5. **Copy or save the QR Code by right-clicking on it.**

    Kaywa gives you the option to use the code's `perma-link` or to copy-paste the HTML code.

Kaywa's generator is a great first stop for the QR Code newbie.

QRStuff.com

QRStuff.com (`www.qrstuff.com`) has an easy-to-use interface (see Figure 3-2) with more options than Kaywa offers.

Figure 3-2: QRStuff.com generates QR Codes in four easy steps.

1. **Select the appropriate Data Type button.**

    This indicates what you want to use the QR Code for (such as a URL, e-mail, phone number, and so on). QRStuff.com gives you some good additional options, such as QR Codes for iTunes links, PayPal purchases, or a vCard.

2. **Enter the content that's appropriate for the data type.**

    If you're prompted to enter a URL, you can enter a URL as is or use its URL shortener, which I recommend.

Using Goo.gl to shorten URLs

The URL for this one, Goo.gl, is strange; I know — but just type it in as you see it! This service from Google generates a trackable, shortened URL and a QR Code all at one site. Follow these steps to use Goo.gl:

The figure above shows an example of Goo.gl.

1. **Type or paste your URL in the text box and click Shorten.**

   You see your URL in the first row of a table below the text box.

2. **To the right of the screen, click the Details link for your URL.**

   A QR Code is automatically created.

3. **Save the image.**

   On a Mac, you can Alt-click the QR Code to copy or save it. On a PC, right-click the QR Code to copy or save it.

   This generator includes free analytics that report scans, country, device, and browser.

The downside of Goo.gl is that you can use it for URLs only. The good news is that it's free and includes analytics. Acknowledging that most QR Codes link to a URL, Goo.gl is a good option.

If you use Google Chrome for a web browser, you can download an extension in the Chrome Web Store that allows you to shorten the current website URL with Goo.gl. With one click you get a shortened URL, a QR Code, and access to analytics. I use the extension and love it!

3. **Choose a foreground color for your QR Code.**

   If you don't plan on using black, read my suggestions in the later section for "Adding Bling to Your QR Code" to spice up your QR Code.

4. **Choose an output type.**

   You have the following choices:

   - **Download:** You can download the QR Code to your computer so you can copy or save it for use.

   - **Print:** You have the option to use label templates to print multiple copies of your QR Code onto standard sheets of Avery round and square stickers. The Avery product code is shown below each label layout.

   - **Email:** Click on this option and you can email your QR Code.

QRStuff.com meets my basic criteria for QR Code generators, but the analytics come only with the paid version. For $11.95 a month, you can see the date, time, location, and device type for scans of as many QR Codes as you can create and use.

Picking the best mobile generator

In Chapter 2, I review some of the better QR Code readers for Apple, Android, and BlackBerry operating systems. Many of these readers can also generate QR Codes.

Generating a code with an app on a mobile device is similar to creating one with their online counterparts Kaywa and QRStuff.com. I use the example of the most popular smartphone on the market, Apple's iPhone, with the free version of QR Reader for iPhone, the most popular QR reader (and generator) in the App Store.

1. **Open QR Reader on your iPhone.**

2. **Touch the QR Code displayed on the bottom left (see Figure 3-3).**

3. **Touch the Creator button, with the wrench icon, at the bottom of the screen (see Figure 3-4).**

4. **Choose the data type and input the requested information.**

   You can see your choices in Figure 3-5.

5. **You then have the choice to rename the QR Code or change the data.**

   Presto! You have a QR Code that you can download to your phone or share via e-mail or on your social networks (see Figure 3-6).

Figure 3-3: Access the QR Code generator by touching the QR Code on the bottom left.

Figure 3-4: Touch the Creator button at the bottom.

Figure 3-5: After choosing the data type, plug in the requested information.

Figure 3-6: After creating your QR Code you can save or share it.

Creating QR Codes with other mobile apps for Apple, Android, and BlackBerry devices involves similar steps and is perfect when you want to use QR Codes on the go.

Getting Help Making Your QR Code

You can easily make your own QR Codes on your computer or mobile device, but if you're planning a marketing campaign that will include a QR Code, you can ask your graphic designer or printer for help creating one.

I'm a belt-and-suspender kind of guy, so if you rely on someone else to create your QR Code, you'll want to make sure they follow the guidelines I outline at the beginning of this chapter. Here's another handy list to follow:

✔ **Make sure the QR Code is a standard size.** You don't want it to be so big or small that it's unsightly or unreadable.

✔ **Review the code generator's capabilities.** Double-check to make sure the QR Code generator they're using will allow you to change the destination of the QR Code, if needed.

✔ **Make sure the QR Code generator can accommodate these four most common data types:** These four include URL, plain text, phone, and SMS (also known as *texting*, which any tween or teenager can explain to you if you're unfamiliar with it).

✔ **Make sure you have the ability to track the QR Code on your own.** It's up to you, not your designer and printer, to track the results of your QR Code campaign.

✔ **Test the code.** Ask your printer to give you a final proof so you can test the QR Code you'll ultimately use. Again, check twice; use once.

Testing Your QR Code

After you create a QR Code, you want to test it before you use it in a campaign, to make sure it's working. Here are some suggestions for testing your QR Code to make sure it works in the real world.

✔ **Scan the QR Code in different lighting.** If it doesn't work, you can increase the contrast of the code (a darker color on a lighter background if you started with something lighter than a black code on a white background) or you can take steps to make sure it's displayed in an area with the right amount of light.

✔ **Try it out on multiple devices.** Scan the code with as many different types of devices — old and new — and QR Code readers as possible to make sure it works.

✔ **Test the code at the distance it will be scanned by people.** Sure, the code works correctly when you scan it on the table in your office. But what about when the QR Code is on a billboard and hundreds of yards from where people will scan it? Will it work then?

✔ **Test Internet access in that area.** Make sure people have Internet access at the very spot at which the code will be scanned. Everyone knows how temperamental mobile and Wi-Fi service can be — one spot might be a dead zone, but ten feet away you might have coverage. It's frustrating but a reality you need to prepare for. Giving people a QR Code with no Internet connection is like giving them a car with no wheels. Using a QR Code at a trade show is a great idea, but not when it's in that part of the exhibit hall that has a notoriously bad Internet connection. You won't know until you try to scan the QR Code at the very spot others will be scanning it.

The bottom line is test, test, test as closely as possible to where, when, and how regular people with ordinary technology will be scanning the QR Code.

Adding Bling to Your QR Code

Most of the QR Codes you see in the real world will be like the QR Codes you see in this book: black squares on white background. But people love to accessorize, and QR Codes are no exception. Here are some easy ways to customize your QR Codes.

✔ **Add some color.** QR Codes don't have to be black and white. They can be any color you want, or multiple colors. You can also use a color gradient without impacting the scanability of the code.

The code itself should be dark and have a light-colored background. The less contrast between the code and the background, the harder it will be to scan. Also, a light color code on a dark background won't work with most scanners.

✔ **Round out those hard edges.** One of the most jarring features of QR Codes is all those hard edges. So rough and cold . . . brrr. Make them more appealing by rounding them out and giving them a softer look (as in Figure 3-7).

Figure 3-7: No hard edges makes for a more appealing QR Code. The palm trees in the middle help too.

✔ **Add some artwork or your logo.** Doing so really turns the QR Code into something other than a bland black-and-white square. It increases the attractiveness of the code and may lead to more scans. You can find QR Code generators online to help you customize your code, or if you're familiar with Photoshop, you can make your own or have a graphic designer make one for you.

I've never used Photoshop, so I searched for an online generator to help me add the logo from my blog, Selfishgiving.com, to a QR Code. Again, I was happy with the code I generated at www.unitaglive.com/qrcode.

It was easy. I just chose a data type (in my case, a URL) and colors, uploaded my logo, and it generated a QR Code for me (see Figure 3-8).

Figure 3-8: Unitag generated this QR Code with my logo and blog colors (red and gray). It took just a couple of minutes.

✔ **Understand error correction.** Up to 30 percent of a QR Code can be used for your artwork or logo without impacting scanability. Some generators allow you to adjust error correction from 0 to 30 percent. The lower the number is, the fewer squares that can be removed to add a logo or artwork. If you set the error correction at 0 percent, removing even one tiny square from the QR Code may render it unscanable. In general, keep error correction above 20 percent if you plan to accessorize your QR Code.

Preparing Your QR Code for the Real World

I've talked a lot about how to correctly generate a QR Code, but where you put that perfectly scanable QR Code after you've created it requires almost as much forethought. Keep these tips in mind:

✔ **Be careful of laminated surfaces.** The reflection can sometimes make the code difficult to read.

✔ **Stick with flat surfaces.** If the QR Code is printed on an object that's uneven, creased, or wrinkled, people will have trouble scanning it.

✔ **Don't make the QR Code too small or big.** Make it just the right size — but at least one square inch — to get the job done. Treat it like the tool it is.

✔ **Keep it simple.** The primary value of a QR Code is what it links to. Overvaluing it is like decorating the handle on a hammer instead of admiring what it can make. Sure, make your codes attractive if you want to. Just remember that the QR Code isn't the Big Show. What it links to is what's interesting, exciting, and valuable.

✔ **Give an explanation.** Tell people what a QR Code is (an offline link to the digital world), what it does (for example, starts a video that shows the strict quality control steps your company uses), and how to access the information on it (such as, download a QR Code reader from your mobile device's app store). See Figure 3-9 for an example.

Figure 3-9: Explain to people what a QR Code is, what it does, and how to use it.

Chapter 4

Linking Your QR Code to Mobile-Friendly Content

*T*he idea of using QR Codes to link the offline world with digital content is "wicked smart," as we like to say in Boston. But just as QR Code creators must give time and thought to generating QR Codes, they also need to consider the mobile content it will link to. If you scan a QR Code and the online content it links to is either difficult to see or use, or both, you'll quickly abandon the effort and move on.

In this chapter, I explain how to adjust online content for mobile devices. I also examine what users want and expect when they scan your QR Code. You may be surprised.

Adapting Content for the Third Screen

The first screen was the television, the second screen was the desktop, and the third screen is the tiny screen found on most portable and mobile devices. (Don't ask me why this list doesn't include the mother of all screens, the movie screen. I guess futurists like things in three.)

Simple, easily navigated, and *compact* are words to live by when creating content for mobile devices. The following sections show you how to adapt your web page for the *tiny screen* and how to meet the expectations of mobile users, which are different from how people view content on desktops, even laptops.

Thinking small

The average screen on a mobile device is just two to slightly more than four inches (measured diagonally). Think how small that is. Your index finger is probably only four inches long. Most screens are smaller (see Figure 4-1).

Figure 4-1: The screen on Apple's iPhone, one of the most popular smartphones in the world, is just 3.5 inches.

Your mobile screen is probably smaller than most mailing labels, but it's amazing what people try to squeeze on this little space, loading it up with nonessential things.

Understanding how content should be viewed on mobile devices requires that you see content in a new way. Here are some ways to start thinking about how content should look on the third screen:

✔ **Whenever possible, use your mobile device for browsing the web.** You'll see sites that are optimized for the mobile screen, but you'll find many that aren't. Doing so can help you define what you want viewers to experience when they see your content on their device.

✔ **Check out different devices.** Try other people's mobile devices so you can see firsthand how their mobile experience might differ from yours.

✔ **Ask mobile users of all ages what they like and don't like about mobile websites.** I asked and found that people older than 50 years of age complained that the site was so cluttered it was difficult to see anything. Younger users complained that bloated sites loaded too slowly.

Mobilizing your website

The screens on mobile devices are small and usually touchscreen. Here are some ways that you can make navigation of your site simpler for those who access it with mobile devices:

✔ **Strip your website down to its core ingredients.** What will people be looking for on your mobile site? It might be different from why they visit your online website (for example, your phone number or address instead of a full product catalog).

✔ **Make buttons larger, as shown in Figure 4-2, and add some space between them.** Don't you hate it when buttons are too small or too close together? Other people hate it too.

✔ **Try to avoid hyperlinks.** They're too small, and hitting the wrong one is too easy.

✔ **Stick with just a couple of your brand's colors to break up the content.** Don't overdo it.

✔ **Optimize the layout for mobile devices.** Users shouldn't have to zoom in to see your mobile page. The QR Code should direct them to a mobile page that needs no tinkering to read, understand, or use.

Regardless of your type of business or size, you can learn by following the practices of an industry leader, such as http://www.amazon.com. Amazon uses the best technology available and sets the standard by which consumers judge other web sites.

Scan the QR Code in the left margin to view Amazon's mobile site and learn from a business superstar.

Figure 4-2: The large buttons on this mobile site are user friendly.

Choosing a plug-in

A lot of websites these days are built using the popular WordPress platform. If this includes yours, you can easily create a mobile website in about 30 seconds (see Figure 4-3).

Figure 4-3: I use WPtouch for my blog.

You can find WPtouch in the WordPress Plugin Directory. Just click on *Install Now*. Here are some advantages to using the plug-in:

- ✔ **It's free!** You can buy a pro version that has more options, but the free version is a great place to start.

- ✔ **It's compatible with the most popular smartphone operating systems.** Sites load easily on Apple, Android, and BlackBerry operating systems.

- ✔ **You can customize its appearance without knowing a lick of code.** WPtouch lets you tweak fonts, header styles, background themes, menus, and more without touching any code.

- ✔ **Users can easily switch between your regular site and your mobile site.** It's as easy as flipping a switch at the bottom of the page.

Another good option to create a mobile version of your site is http://www.dudamobile.com, which has a free and paid version. The free version gives you templates to choose from, the ability to resize images, and even buttons for users to call or text you. I tried the service with my own blog and was impressed that my mobile site included my banner image and several perfectly sized photos.

Take precautions. Before installing any plug-in, be sure to back up your site just in case something goes wrong.

Using fewer images

Images are great way to communicate a message, but stick with just one or two. The more images on your site, the longer it will take for the page to load — a delay that may prompt the user to look elsewhere.

Using just a couple images highlights the importance of seeing your site through the eyes of the mobile viewer. Lots of images may be perfect for your traditional site, but those same images on a mobile device will be a disaster for viewers.

Keep the following guidelines in mind as you resize photos:

✔ In general, use images or graphics as little as possible. If you must, stick with a jpeg, gif or png format because they take the least amount of time to load.

✔ Make sure the pictures are compressed and users don't have the option to view a larger image. Doing so slows down the site.

✔ An industry practice tags images in case users have images turned off. Tagging the image with text tells the user what they're missing.

Many websites use Flash, a multimedia platform made by Adobe, to add animation and video to web pages. Flash isn't a good idea for mobile sites. Do yourself and your mobile users a favor: dump Flash. Flash doesn't even work on Apple's popular devices. Operating systems that Flash does work on — Android and BlackBerry — require an extra click or two to start the video.

If you're not experienced in the latest web standards for mobile browsers, which includes HTML5, use one of the popular video sharing services such as Youtube or Vimeo to share videos on mobile devices.

Being careful with form fields

Imagine this: You scan a QR Code to apply for a product refund. Wow, what a great way to do it! Your heart sinks though when you see that you ended up on a regular web page with a dozen or more tiny boxes to fill in. That's a terrible waste of a good QR Code. Fortunately, you can optimize form fields for mobile devices (see Figure 4-4).

Two options for creating mobile forms are Google Docs and Formstack (www.formstack.com).

Delivering an app-like experience

Apps are a great model of how users want to consume mobile content. Apps are easy to use, have large buttons, few images, no Flash, and use mobile-friendly form fields.

Figure 4-4: Like websites, form fields need to be adapted for the mobile viewer.

People like apps. More than 400,000 apps are available for just Android operating systems. Mobile users like apps because they deliver the type of experience people want and expect on their phones.

Taking the extra step to create an app for your website may not be necessary if your mobile site looks and works like one.

✔ Start by sketching out on paper or in Google Drawings how your mobile site will flow from point A to point B.

✔ Try a lot of different apps to see how they work. You'll notice that the best ones have a common user experience that you should build into your mobile site. Shortening the learning curve makes for happier users.

✔ Let people try a beta version of your mobile site. Just watch them, don't show or tell them anything. You'll gain some valuable insights when you see satisfaction or frustration on their faces.

Before going live with your mobile site, test it on `mobile grader.com` and `mobilemoxie.com`. Mobile Grader analyzes your website, grades it on several mobile friendly metrics, and tells you how to get a better grade. At Mobile Moxie click on *Handset Emulators* on the navigation bar, enter your website, and you can see how it will look on different smartphones.

Boston's Emerson College delivers an app like experience with its mobile site. Scan the QR Code in the left margin to view it.

Giving Mobile Viewers What They Want, Expect

Just as people expect mobile sites to be as functional as apps, they have preferences on what mobile sites should deliver. Keep that in mind when you're choosing what your QR Code will link to.

In 2011, a survey of 415 smartphone users by marketing firm MGH in Baltimore, Maryland, showed that consumers would scan a QR Code for these reasons.

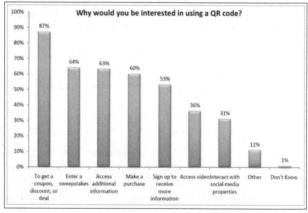

Figure 4-5: Why would you be interested in using a QR Code?

Meeting user expectations for what QR Codes should link to can increase your chances for success. It gives users a predictable outcome with a new technology, perhaps reinforcing the value of scanning QR Codes in the first place.

Chapter 5

Making Sure Your QR Code Is Scanned

• •

In This Chapter

▶ Telling people about your QR Code

▶ Improving the chances your QR Code is scanned

▶ Giving people good reasons to keep on scanning

• •

*T*he goal of this book is to show you how to use QR Codes for marketing and make them a successful, permanent part of your marketing plan. I want to make sure you and I are clear on our terms.

QR Codes are two-dimensional barcodes that link the offline world with digital content. The things you do to get and keep stakeholders is called *marketing*. The specific tactics you adopt to realize your marketing objectives are part of your *marketing plan*.

In this chapter, I show you how to promote your QR Code with stakeholders, how to increase the odds they'll scan it, and, finally, how to add value with your QR Code so that, after someone's scanned it, they're happy they did.

Spreading the Word on Your QR Code

Your first challenge is getting people to take notice of your QR Code. Believe it or not, you could start with a QR Code itself. That's the logic behind some of the huge QR Codes you see in places such as Times Square. They get people to take notice by making the code so big and omnipresent that people are sure to talk and ask questions about it.

I'm not suggesting you find a billboard space in Times Square, but a large QR Code at the entrance to your office or your reception area may be just what you need (see Figure 5-1).

Figure 5-1: This QR Code says it all: "Scan me!"

Here are nine more ideas for promoting your QR Code:

- ✔ **Put a code at the bottom of your e-mail signature.** Someone is bound to ask, "What the heck is that?"

- ✔ **Give some instructions.** Explain what a QR Code is and how to scan one in your blog, website, and e-mail news-letter. Take responsibility for educating your audience on what the codes are and how to use them.

- ✔ **Use them in your advertising.** Put QR Codes in all your advertisements so people get used to seeing them con-nected with your organization.

- ✔ **Include a QR Code on your business card (see Figure 5-2).** You can link it to your phone number, your Linkedin page, a video, a newspaper story profiling you, or your involvement in a recent project.

Ordering QR Codes in bulk

After reading this book and creating and using QR Codes, you may decide you really like QR Codes — a lot. You don't want just one QR Code; you want hundreds of them!

Infatuation may not be your only motivation. Maybe you're planning a conference and want QR Codes on attendees' name tags so you can track attendance to different breakout sessions. Attendees can also scan them to swap contact information.

The good news is that you can process all these QR Codes in bulk. QRStuff.com, one of the QR Code–generator services I recommend in Chapter 3, is just one company that can process hundreds of QR Codes at once. For most services, this involves uploading a simple Excel file or other data file, to their site. Be aware that many sites charge a fee for processing QR Codes in bulk.

However, if you want to generate a bunch of QR Codes for free and you don't mind inputting the data, try the bulk generator at www. qrexplore.com. You simply enter the data for as many QR Codes as you like — each on a new line — and click the Submit Query button. You can download all the codes you created into a zip file for easy use.

Figure 5-2: Business cards are a popular place for QR Codes.

✔ **Train everyone on your team to talk about QR Codes with everyone they meet.** Remember, talk is cheap. They should know how to scan and use one too.

✔ **Affix QR Codes to all the products in your store.** Over time, give each code a personalized link to interesting and useful content.

✔ **Add QR Codes to your presentation and slides.** Regardless of your speaking topic, take a moment to explain what they are and how to scan them.

✔ **Give QR Codes a prominent place at your events.** Include them on table signs, drink coasters, place settings, and even napkins.

✔ **Spread the word.** Tell the real busybodies in your neighborhood about QR Codes — they'll be sure to tell everyone.

Making It Easy for People to Scan Your QR Code

A key part in getting someone to do anything is not giving him or her an excuse to say no. If you pitch a potential client and he's really interested, but you never call him back or return his messages, you're just giving the prospect an excuse to say no and buy from someone else.

The same applies to QR Codes. You have to make scanning and using QR Codes just as easy as possible. This is especially true given that a study in 2011 reported that three of ten consumers don't understand QR Codes. You and I have our work cut out for us.

The following sections give some of the reasons why people may say no to QR Codes and what you can do to turn that no into a yes.

They don't know what that funny-looking, black-and-white square is

People are asking what that funny-looking, black-and-white square is a lot because they're seeing them everywhere, usually with little or no explanation of what to do with them. Here's how you can introduce QR Codes to people who aren't familiar with them:

✔ **Share some details.** Include text near the code that tells people (as shown in Figure 5-3) what the QR Code can deliver when they scan it. Here's an example of the text that might accompany a QR Code in your marketing materials: "For our weekly specials, visit our website or scan this QR Code with your mobile device."

People are more likely to try QR codes — or anything for that matter — when they're instructed on how to do it and are clear on what they'll get in return.

Scan this special code using a QR reader on your smartphone and visit stores.LEGO.com to stay up to date on the latest LEGO Store news and events!

Figure 5-3: This QR Code shows and tells.

✔ **Think about placement.** Large QR Codes on billboards get people thinking, "Where will it take me if I scan it?" But if surprise isn't your angle, put QR Codes in places where people can connect the dots on what they link to. A QR Code on a takeout menu will probably link to an online menu or app. It makes sense, right? There's a good case to be made for putting QR Codes in predict-able spots where people will connect the dots — literally and figuratively — and use them. See Figure 5-4 for an example of a simple and clever placement of a QR Code.

✔ **Address performance anxiety head-on.** People like to try new things, but not when they may come off looking like a fool. Put QR Codes in a practical place and not some-where where bystanders will question a person's sanity. QR Codes on register signs may seem like a good idea, but not when people have to put on a show for everyone behind them to download the reader, scan the code, and so on. People don't want to look foolish if they can't figure it out, so instead they don't try. You can still have QR Codes in the checkout line, but how about toward the back of the line so shoppers can try it while they're waiting?

Figure 5-4: Hmmm. I get the sense that this QR Code is where I could get a question answered.

✔ **Give people a good reason to scan.** Refer to the end of Chapter 4, where I list the main reasons people scan QR Codes now and what they plan to scan them for tomorrow and after. A recently launched website focused on poking fun at QR code failures shares many examples of QR Codes that just aren't scan worthy. Scan the QR code in the left margin to visit this site.

✔ **Give people another option.** The important thing about any kind of marketing is that it accomplishes your goals. The QR Code is just a tool, and sometimes it may not be the right one or you may need to use it with something else to get the job done. That's why many good QR Code marketing campaigns give users an alternative to scanning, such as a URL or text code. A wise man once said that people don't want a drill, they want a hole. Give people *what they want*.

They don't know how to scan them

Many people are curious about QR Codes and want to use them, but they just don't know how. And, unfortunately, they're not getting a lot of help. Here's how you can change that.

> ✔ **Direct people to a reader.** Most QR Codes have a short message underneath them, like this one: "Visit your app store to download a QR reader." Until QR Codes become well known and native to mobile devices, you'll need to tell people how to unlock the content.

> ✔ **Educate frontline staff.** If someone asks, your staff needs to know what a QR Code is, what its value to the user, and how to scan it. If employees can't tell people why and how they should scan a QR Code, you're missing a powerful opportunity to woo potential adopters.

> Scan the QR Code in the left margin and read an excellent case study about specialty earphone maker Etymotic. They realized the competitive-edge QR Codes delivered and made staff training a top priority.

The QR Code doesn't work

The last thing you want is someone scanning your QR Code and then being disappointed when it doesn't work. In addition to the best practices I outline in Chapter 3 for creating QR Codes, follow these three tips:

> ✔ **Make sure your QR Codes are at least one-by-one inch.** Some older mobile devices can't read codes smaller than this.

> ✔ **Make sure to use a URL shortener.** If you embed a long URL on your QR Code, you'll increase the chance that the code will be "too busy" and won't scan. Shortening the URL produces a cleaner code that's easily read. Three popular URL shorteners are TinyURL.com, Goo.gl, and Bitly.

> ✔ **Make sure your QR Code has a *quiet zone*.** This is the white area around the actual code that separates the code from what's around it (shown in Figure 5-5).

If you're using one of the QR Code generators I recommended in Chapter 3, the QR Code you create will come with a 4mm border that you shouldn't block or reduce. Every QR Code is unique piece of digital art. Don't ruin it by removing the frame.

White Area = Quiet Zone

Figure 5-5: Note the white area around the actual code. It's called the *quiet zone.*

Adding Value with QR Codes

The question is whether QR Codes are the right tool for the job. Do they get the job done? Do they add value to the project? Ask yourself these two questions before embarking on any marketing campaign that involves QR Codes:

Here are a few more suggestions:

- ✔ **The code should do one thing.** This point seems easy because creating a QR Code requires you enter one data point (a URL, phone number, map, YouTube video, and so on). But are you really directing the user to one thing? Using a QR Code to open a website is one thing, but not if it takes the user to a page with too many options. You might be better off directing them to a certain page on your website. If you run an auto dealership and your QR Code dials a phone number, where does it go — sales, parts, service? Drill down to that *one thing* you want your QR Code to accomplish.

✔ **Consider the context.** If you want to use your QR Code to give your customers a coupon for apples, where should you place the QR Code — at the apple bin in the aisles or at the register? In the aisles is probably a better option, because the line at the register is generally hectic, and the shopper may have forgotten what the QR Code is for. Context matters. Strive to think like your audience.

✔ **Be relevant.** Lately, whenever I get a phone book delivered to my house, I notice the cover often has a QR Code on it so I can download the phone book app on my mobile device (see Figure 5-6). This is smart, because I'm usually halfway to the recycling barrel when I see it. The phone book company is trying to connect with mobile-savvy customers who will quickly dispose of the paper phone book but may want a mobile option. The QR Code delivers a viable alternative that I might not have considered if I hadn't seen it.

Figure 5-6: The QR Code on this phone book opens a mobile app.

✔ **Move the user down the funnel.** You know what they say: "If you're not closing, you're in customer service, not sales." Your QR Code should move your customer closer to buying. If I run a wine company and I put QR Codes on my wine bottles, what should they link to? My website? Or would I be better off linking it to customer reviews of my wines? Or how about a pairing of the wine with recipes? Which one is more likely to *close the sale*? Fortunately, you can track each strategy and see which QR Code is most effective in moving the consumer to buy.

✔ **Enhance the experience.** This suggestion is my most important takeaway on using QR Codes. The code should do something different, something that the thing it's on *can't do*. Give it a real purpose. For example, if you put a QR Code on your resume that links to a PDF version of your resume, that's a terrible waste of a QR Code. The person has your resume. They probably don't need a version of it on their phone. Instead, use the QR Code to link users to your recommendations on LinkedIn. Or how about a QR Code that opens a YouTube video of you giving a speech on a topic of interest to a potential employer?

QR Codes require the same forethought and discretion that PowerPoint demands. Just as you use visuals to complement your spoken message and not just repeat yourself, use your QR Code to communicate something that can't be said.

Chapter 6

Measuring Your Success with a Code-Management System

. . . .

In This Chapter

▶ Making the case for tracking QR Codes

▶ Picking a QR Code management system

▶ Analyzing the data

. . . .

*Y*ou should track QR Codes for the same reason you track visits to your website: to know where you're inbound links are coming from. With QR Codes, you can track the number of daily scans, each scan's location, and what types of mobile devices scanned the code. This data can help you better develop and execute QR Code campaigns.

In this chapter, I explain why to track your QR Codes, how to track them using either your QR Code generator or URL shortener, and how to make sense of the data after you have it.

Understanding Why You Should Track QR Codes

To paraphrase Mark Twain, the only thing worse than the person who doesn't understand the value of QR Code analytics is the person who does but still doesn't use them.

If you're one of these persons, you don't need to worry. I'm here to help with some reasons that can hopefully replace your uncertainty with education or hesitation with purpose.

- ✔ **You can't improve what you can't measure.** If you don't have a basic metric, such as how many people scanned your code, how can you know if your code is doing the job you intended?

- ✔ **You can track location.** When your QR Code is scanned around the country or around the world, you can tell where it was scanned and on what mobile device. For example, in Figure 6-1 you can see the report I received for a QR Code I generated through uQR.me. The report shows in what countries and cities the code was scanned and with what types of devices. This kind of data can help you tailor your marketing campaigns to account for regional adoption, language, and technology.

- ✔ **You know what's hot or not.** This allows you to adapt campaigns as needed and to discover what truly works with your target audience.

- ✔ **You can experiment.** For example, you can embed a URL in one QR Code and a phone number in another to gauge what data point your audience prefers most.

- ✔ **You can figure out what kind of mobile device is primarily scanning your QR Code and optimize the content for that device.** For example, if the device is an older Apple 3G smartphone, you can create a very basic mobile page without images that loads quickly.

- ✔ **It's free!** Many good analytic tools for QR Codes are powerful and free. Paid versions are also available and generally come with a reader and generator. Why wouldn't you track your QR Code?

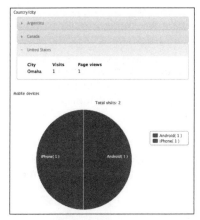

Figure 6-1: I track these two data points for QR Codes in this book: location and mobile device.

Choosing a Tracking System

You have two choices for tracking a QR Code: You can use the analytical tools that come with most QR Code generators (see Chapter 3) or you can use a URL shortener service such as Bitly or Goo.gl to track your code.

The main advantage of using the tracking system that comes with a QR Code generator site — such as QRStuff.com, or the one I use in this chapter, uQR.me — is that you can track any data type you want (such as URL, vCard, or phone number), whereas a URL shortener service tracks only a URL.

However, the difference between generators and shorteners isn't so great when you realize that most people use QR Codes with URLs anyway.

Regardless of which tracking system you choose, here's a short primer on how to use both.

Using a generator

A *generator site* is where you can create and design your very own QR Code. Most QR Code generators come with tracking tools. Sometimes they're free, but sometimes not. Make sure to check your generator for analytics before you create and use a QR Code in a campaign.

The QR Code–management system I use for this book — and in my previous book, *Cause Marketing For Dummies* — is uQR. me. I purchased the Campaigns account (for $50 per year) and pay just $1 per QR Code.

Many other QR Code–tracking services, including those I mention in Chapter 3, have similar management systems that give the same data and work the same way as uQR.me. To this list I would add, delivr.com, a free QR Code generator and tracker.

After I create and use a QR Code, I visit uQR.me, log in, pick the QR Code I want statistics for, and complete these steps:

1. **Click the Statistics link (see Figure 6-2).**

Figure: 6-2: Tracking QR Codes on uQR.me.

You can filter the results by date and see the daily analytics (see Figure 6-3).

2. **Click to see a chart of the number of scans on each day.**

You can view what country and cities the scans came from, as shown in Figure 6-4.

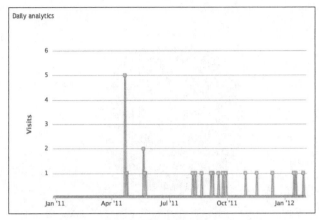

Figure 6-3: You can see how many times your QR Code was scanned and on which days.

3. Click to see the locations of the scans.

Figure 6-4: Scans from around the country and the world.

You can see which mobile devices were used, as shown in Figure 6-5.

4. Click to find out what types of mobile devices scanned your code.

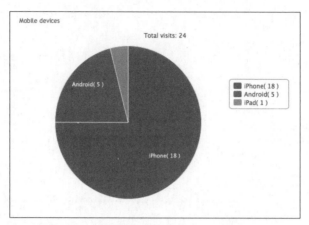

Figure 6-5: iPhone followed by Android and Apple's iPad.

Using a URL shortener

A *URL shortener* is often for services such as Twitter where
the number of characters matter. However, the value of a
URL shortener for QR Codes has to do with density. Because
the URL is encoded within the black modules that comprise a
QR Code, the longer the URL the denser the QR code and the
more difficult it is to decode with a reader. A shorter QR Code
means fewer black modules and an easier, faster scan.

Here's how to create and track a QR Code with the popular
URL shortener service Bitly:

1. **Go to** http://bitly.com.

2. **Type the web address you want to shorten (for exam-
   ple,** http://www.fordummies.com) **in the Shorten
   Links Here text box and click Shorten, as shown in
   Figure 6-6.**

   The shortened link appears below the text box.

3. **Click the Info Page+ link.**

   On the right, you'll see a QR Code with the shortened
   link under it that you can now use for your campaign.

During the campaign, visit Bitly to track your QR Code. Check out the next section to know what to do the data.

Figure 6-6: Visit Bitly, shorten your URL, and click Info Page+.

Making Sense of the Data

You have used either a QR Code generator or URL shortener. You collect some data from your tracking efforts and wonder, "What do I do with it now? How do I make sense of this info to improve my QR Code campaigns?" This section is for you. Take a look at the types of analytics that QR Code–management systems deliver and how to best use them:

- ✓ **Total visits:** This metric shows you the total number of scans of your QR Code. It's the basis for determining the success of your QR Code. The more scans you have means the more visitors to your chosen destination, which means the better chance the user will take the action you intended (for example, learning more about your company, buying a product, watching a video, or booking a time for a service).

- ✓ **Daily visits:** Analyze daily visits in context and uncover what's really driving them and how you can expand on the success. Was your QR Code scanned on weekends, or weekdays, or only one specific day? Be open minded in your analysis. Consumers may be scanning more QR Codes on the days when your best staff is showing them how.

✔ **Country and city:** Are you wondering in what countries
and cities your QR Code is scanned? Tracking services
can tell you. Use this data to expand your QR Code use in
areas where scans are greatest. Although the sample size
is small in Figure 6-7, New York City has always been a
hotbed for new technologies. If your business has a pres-
ence there or in other major cities, expand your use of
QR Codes in New York and other major markets.

Most tracking systems also show you the number of *page
views* (which you can also see in Figure 6-7), the number of
pages on your mobile site that the user viewed after scanning the code. More page views than visits indicate that the
user visited another page. The first page the user lands on is
counted as one page view. If the user touches a button to visit
another page, that's two page views, and so on. In Figure 6-7,
you can see that in Denver there were two visits to the page
that the QR Code links to, and then one visitor clicked a link
to another page on my site. Although more page views generally signals greater user interest, having to scroll down page
after page is also annoying for many mobile users. Use as few
pages as possible to get them to take the desired action.

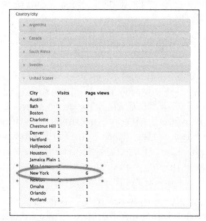

Figure 6-7: Tracking shows country, city, visits, and page views.

✔ **Device used.** Knowing what device your QR Code was
scanned with helps you optimize mobile content for
Apple, Android, or BlackBerry operating systems. Keep

in mind that studies show that QR Codes are scanned overwhelmingly (more than 60 percent) on iPhones. Android is second, and BlackBerry a distant third. Even though your pages should be optimized for all three devices, focusing on Apple users isn't a bad idea. To see how your mobile content will look on other devices, use your favorite search engine to look up *mobile emulators.*

Scanning and grocery shopping at the same time

One company that is already seeing the future of QR Codes for purchases is Internet grocer Peapod, which is available in 24 U.S. cities. Hoping to capitalize on the needs of the busy consumer that spends, on average, 2.5 hours a week commuting to work, Peapod is buying ad space at commuter stops in Philadelphia pitching commuters on grocery shopping (see the following figure that shows where you can scan the QR Code to download the grocer's app and then shop).

But instead of using the QR Code for direct purchases, the code on the display downloads the grocer's smartphone app. Shoppers then have the choice of scanning the items on the ads, or browsing thousands of items featured in the app — just as they would in the bricks-and-mortar grocery store.

(continued)

(continued)

After you enter your credit card information in the Peapod app, it's stored for later use. Using apps to pay for products and services purchased on mobile devices will probably be the next step for U. S. consumers, as they feel comfortable shopping and paying within apps.

However, it won't be long before shoppers are bypassing the extra step of downloading an app and just scanning and paying in just a couple clicks. But even here QR Codes could play a key role.

Chapter 7

Exploring Possible Uses for QR Codes

*Q*R Codes have a place in every business, every industry, and every part of your life where you have a need to connect the offline world with digital content.

This chapter looks at how nonprofit organizations can use QR Codes for fundraising, teachers for the classroom, professionals for furthering their careers, and finally, people of all ages for fun and adventure.

Of course, QR Codes have many other uses. I'm confident that the ideas I share in this chapter can spur their use in ways that you or I never considered. That's what's exciting about QR Codes. They can enhance passions, further learning, and increase success and enjoyment of the tangible world around us.

Using QR Codes for Education

Schools and classrooms are great places for QR Codes. These days, people learn as much on the web as they do in the classroom. QR Codes are the perfect bridge between the two.

Another advantage of QR Codes in education is the receptive audience that's waiting for them. A recent study by the Dachis Group showed that 81 percent of college students own smartphones. Young people are *early adopters:* They embrace new technologies easily, eagerly, and more quickly than others.

QR Codes in education are like a square, black-and-white petri dish that students will examine and study. Soon teachers and other people will be marveling at their growth in schools around the world.

Here are some ways that administrators, teachers, and students can start experimenting with QR Codes.

For administrators

The administrators at my schools — admittedly a few years back — were all about order, communication, and efficiency. QR Codes could have helped them do their jobs better. That's why I'm happy to suggest these ways for the modern, smartphone-toting administrator.

- ✓ **Get feedback.** Link a QR Code to a poll or feedback page so students, teachers, and parents can ask questions, share comments, and make complaints.

- ✓ **Get fast action.** Post a QR Code in trouble spots in the school so you can instantly get a text when a problem arises.

- ✓ **Audio tours.** Put QR Codes along a guided tour of the school so visitors can listen to audio and watch videos.

- ✓ **Information desk.** Put QR Codes where students frequently have questions. Scan the code, and it sends a text to someone who can answer questions.

- ✓ **Give directions.** Place a QR Code at the entrance to your school that links to a Google map of the surrounding area.

- ✓ **Hand out grades.** Use a password-protected QR Code for report cards and progress reports sent home to parents.

For teachers or professors

I taught undergraduates in the early 1990s before QR Codes were invented. But even then I craved for a technology that would be bridge between students and me. If I were still teaching today, this is how I would use them.

- ✔ **For meetings.** Put a QR Code on your office door and link it to an online calendar such as Tungle (at www.tungle. me) so students can check your availability and book a date and time.

- ✔ **Share your vCard.** Put a QR Code on the chalkboard or in your syllabus the first day of class so that smartphone-toting students can capture and store your contact information.

- ✔ **Pique curiosity.** Use the QR Code treasure hunt generator at ClassTools.net (at http://classtools.net/QR) to create QR Codes with questions and answers and post them all around your classroom or school (see Figure 7-1).

Figure 7-1: Hang QR Codes throughout your classroom. Have students scan them and answer the question for extra credit.

✔ **Enhance the value of textbooks and handouts.** Put QR Codes on or in the textbook or on handouts to point students to additional resources.

✔ **Reduce student excuses.** Use a QR Code to add important dates to their calendars. "I know it's on your calendar. I put it there." That's a priceless response to "I forgot."

✔ **Ask questions and get answers.** Link a QR Code to Quora (at www.quora.com), the online question-and-answer site, where students can see answers to frequently asked questions and can also submit questions. You or other members of the class will be notified of posted questions and can answer them.

✔ **Get their attention.** Post a large QR Code in the classroom offering extra credit to students who scan it and answer a question.

✔ **Access Wi-Fi.** Are you sick of telling students how to log onto the classroom's Wi-Fi? Use a QR Code to link them directly to the login page.

For students

Students are probably the best candidates to actually use QR Codes. They're digitally-savvy, smartphone-equipped, and eager for as little interaction as possible with teachers and professors. QR Codes in the classroom belong more to them than anyone else.

✔ **Invest in a QR Code stamp.** Use it on everything you turn in so your teacher always has your name and contact information.

✔ **Share your notes.** Forward a QR Code to a friend to give her online access to your class notes.

✔ **Make some extra money.** Put your QR Code on bulletin boards that link readers to tutoring sessions with you.

✔ **Add depth to presentations.** Show your teacher and your class you did your research. Give them the option on your slides of scanning a QR Code for more information.

✔ **Test yourself.** Put QR Codes on objects like stones or bones on a skeleton that will test your knowledge of the names and function.

✓ **Organize study groups.** Hand out QR Codes in class with information on the date and location of the next study group.

✓ **Party time.** Celebrate the weekend in style. Include a QR Code on your next party invite with the time, location, and your phone number.

Using QR Codes for Fundraising

I'm really excited about the potential for QR Code use for causes, especially for fundraising. I have a special interest in the area, because I've spent my adult life working for nonprofits and raising money. I used QR Codes before they became hot and trendy, so I've been sold on the value of them for some time. Here's my take on the benefits of QR Codes for causes and my particular area of nonprofit work, cause marketing.

Cause marketing isn't just the marketing of causes. I define it as the partnership of a nonprofit and for-profit for mutual profit. To discover more, you can check out my other book, *Cause Marketing For Dummies,* or visit my blog at www.selfish giving.com.

✓ **Tell your story.** Nonprofits can tell their stories in several different ways with QR Codes. They can link to pictures, video, testimonials, and so on that can better share the nonprofit's mission with key stakeholders.

✓ **Make a donation.** QR Codes can link donors to a donation page where they can support your cause.

Most QR Code generators, including QRstuff.com and uQR.me, which I recommend in this book, give you the option to encode a Paypal buy-now link.

✓ **Educate your visitor.** If you run a museum or historical site, QR Codes can bring artwork, statutes, furniture, armaments, and even gravesites to life by sharing behind-the-scenes details about their origin, use, or restoration.

✓ **Scan the cause.** Are you an activist trying to share your message with demonstrators? Brand your signage with QR Codes so people can access directions for the march or learn more about the cause.

✔ **Like this.** Nonprofits are always looking for ways to get more Facebook Likes. Try putting a QR Code in your newsletter or display one at your next event so supporters can show they love you with a like.

✔ **Save money on your summer mailing.** The United States Postal Service will offer a 3 percent discount on first-class and standard mail pieces, as well as flats and cards, during July and August, 2012, if they include a QR Code. You get the discount upfront, and the only requirement is that the code has to relate to some part of the mailing.

The USPS is driving adoption of QR Codes! In summer 2011, nearly 40 percent of mailing pieces had QR Codes or other approved bar codes.

✔ **Sign a petition.** A QR Code can link supporters to a page where they can find out more about your goals and sign their name to an online petition.

✔ **Take action.** Local governments can increase their responsiveness to community concerns with a QR Code that connects them immediately with an official.

✔ **Be transparent.** Consumers frequently complain that nonprofits aren't transparent enough on where their dollars are going. Use a QR Code at the point of donation to show donors their support in action.

✔ **Answer a question.** Cause products that support nonprofits with a percentage or portion of sales can feature a QR Code that links to a frequently asked questions page where donors can get questions answered about the campaign, how much money the nonprofit will receive, and so on.

For more information on this charitable program, scan with smartphone QR reader.

Figure 7-2: In one fundraiser I linked a QR Code to the question and answer site Quora where donors could discover more about cause marketing.

✔ **Embrace innovation.** I've worked at many nonprofits that do good work but lag on putting the latest technologies to good use. QR Codes are bound to what will probably be the most dominant screen in history: the small screen on mobile devices. This is your opportunity to be the early adopters in one of biggest technological revolutions of our time.

✔ **Say thank you.** A friend of mine supports a local school, and every time she makes a gift, the school includes a QR Code on the thank-you letter, with a personal thank-you video from a student.

Using Give.mobi for mobile giving

The day will soon come when you'll simply be able to press a button on your mobile device to donate to a good cause. Until then, QR Codes may be the best option for mobile giving, especially for cause marketing partnerships between a business and nonprofit. Leading the charge in this area is Tulsa, Oklahoma–based CharityCall and a service called Give.mobi. Give.mobi is probably the best option out there right now for mobile giving. Here's how Give.mobi works.

1. **Shoppers scan a QR Code that takes them to a custom giving page.**

   The QR Code can appear anywhere: on a register sign or product, in a sales flier, and so on. Check out this QR Code appeal from Cinnabon bakeries (see Figure 7-3).

Figure 7-3: This QR Code appeared on Cinnabon register signs.

The first page highlights the details of the program, in Cinnabon's case a fundraiser for antihunger organization Share Our Strength (see Figure 7-4). Users can also easily share the campaign with friends on Twitter and Facebook.

Figure 7-4: The first mobile page shares details and makes sharing easy.

2. **Tap Give Now to visit the donation page (see Figure 7-5).**

   If you're uneasy about making a donation on your phone, you can make a pledge by entering an amount and e-mail address so you can receive a link to donate via PayPal, credit card, or debit card.

   One of the advantages of mobile giving over text giving is that you can donate any amount you want. Text gifts are usually limited to either five or ten dollars.

   After you enter a gift amount and tap Give Now, you're asked to sign in to your PayPal account, as shown in Figure 7-6, and make a gift. Of course, the process isn't as easy if you don't have a PayPal account.

Give.mobi isn't free. There's a small set-up fee, and donations are subject to a five percent management fee. You have to decide if you can live with that expense, but I believe it's modest.

Figure 7-5: You pick the amount you want to donate.

Figure 7-6: Sign into your PayPal to complete your transaction.

Here's the million dollar question: Does this new mobile platform work? It can. Check out the nearby sidebar for more nitty gritty about Cinnabon's fundraiser.

Give.mobi will have plenty of competition as other mobile giving platforms are rolled out. Mobile is the future, and perhaps the future of giving. Keep your eyes peeled for new developments.

More than just sweet rolls: Raising money with QR Codes

I was impressed that Cinnabon raised $3,800 for Share Our Strength in just five days. The average donation was $43, and the average cost per donation was $3.40.

Cinnabon president Kat Cole is a believer: "The ability to reach out and allow patrons to donate using their mobile smartphones made a big difference."

Like the legends of white whales that inspired Herman Melville to write *Moby-Dick,* we'll have to chase down each new mobile development for fundraising to see if it's real or fake. But Cinnabon's success with Share Our Strength proves that Give. mobi isn't just another fish story.

Using QR Codes for Your Career

QR Codes are a great way to help you find a job or further your career. If you're on the other side of the desk and looking to hire someone, QR Codes may even help you find your next employee!

Don't just slap a QR Code on anything to look smart and cool. You have to know what it does and be able to explain its use and value to someone else. Remember, using QR Codes is about making things better, not worse. Your career is serious business.

If you're confident in your intentions and knowledge of QR Codes, here are a few ways to make it a regular part of your professional life.

- ✔ **Include one on your resume.** Just make sure it doesn't link to an online version of your resume (a major QR Code fail!). Use the QR Code to link to your About.me page, your recommendations on LinkedIn, or a YouTube video of you speaking at an industry event.

- ✔ **Schedule a meeting.** Put QR Codes on your resume and business card that link potential employers to your Tungle online calendar, where they can easily check your availability to meet and book a date and time.

✔ **Be different.** In the employment section of your local newspaper, place an ad with just a QR Code that links to a page with details on your work interests and background. This idea is especially good if you're looking for work in new media or technology. Employers in these fields will recognize the QR Code and the opportunity it holds.

Using QR Codes is all about knowing your audience and their openness to new technologies. Use QR Codes when they're appropriate and relevant — not just because they're cool.

✔ **Use them on job postings.** Interested candidates can scan the QR Code for details and even save it for viewing later. Here's another way to use the code: Record the hiring manager talking about the position and the type of candidate she's looking for, and link the code to the video.

✔ **Reduce disruptions.** Are people constantly asking you for the same things all the time? Hang QR Codes on your door with answers to frequently asked questions so you can get some work done!

✔ **Fix things.** Don't you hate when something breaks in the office (maybe a printer, copier, or fax machine) and you can never find instructions on how to fix it? Encode them on a QR Code that can be affixed right to front of the equipment.

✔ **Take ownership of a project.** Let your boss know you worked on something by stamping your own personal QR Code on key papers and projects. Get the credit you deserve and earn it in a savvy way.

✔ **Submit a video resume.** A video resume is when you use a face and a voice to share your background and work experience. This strategy isn't for everyone, but it certainly can get you noticed (see Figure 7-7).

Remember when using video that people have short attention spans and don't want to watch you feed your cat for twenty minutes. Keep your video brief and focused on the task at hand.

✔ **Be cool.** Looking to hire young people to work in your store or restaurant? Include QR Codes in your job postings at career fairs and college campuses. Let candidates know you are as hip as they are.

Figure 7-7: A video resume triggered by a QR Code just might be the thing that gets an employer's attention.

Your personal information belongs to you. If you're concerned about sharing private information with a QR Code, some generators allow password protection (as shown in Figure 7-8), so you can control who sees it.

Change QRlink | **Download QR** | Privacy Settings | **Statistics**

I want to share my QRlink with:

○ Everybody
◉ People I decide. QRlink is password-protected
○ uQR.me friends only

Choose a password

Password   •••••••••••

Repeat password   •••••••••••

SAVE CHANGES

Figure 7-8: Many QR Code generators, such as uQR.me, the one I use, give you the option of protecting your QR Code with a password.

Using QR Codes for Fun and Adventure

You can also use QR Codes to make work more fun — and easier too. Or you can use QR Codes away from work to just have fun.

- ✔ **Make moving easier.** Put QR Codes on moving boxes that link to a list of items in each box. Think about how much easier this would make retrieving boxes from storage and unpacking.

- ✔ **Add them to your invites.** Give your party invite an interesting twist with a QR Code that provides guests a preview of the special evening you have planned.

- ✔ **Have a QR Code scavenger hunt.** Spread QR Codes around your neighborhood or town giving clues of where to find the next clue and win the hunt.

- ✔ **Have a QR Code party.** Invite a bunch of new friends over and let them make their own QR Codes that reveal something special about themselves.

- ✔ **Preserve holiday memories.** Keep special memories on a holiday ornament adorned with a QR Code (see Figure 7-9).

Figure 7-9: An ornament with QR Code.

- ✔ **Find your pet.** Thousands of pets go missing every day in this country. Increase the odds that you'll find yours by adding a QR Code to its collar that links to your phone number, email or other contact information.

- ✔ **Keep track of plantings.** Tag plants, shrubs, and trees with durable QR Codes that give you watering, disease, and care information. Open your garden to tours and let visitors leave their own reviews of their favorite blooms.

- ✔ **Track your family history.** Add QR Codes to pictures, letters, and documents to enrich their meaning with audio interviews and remembrances, video, or pictures that tell a story.

 Scan the QR Code in the left margin to see a fabulous QR Code campaign called *The World Park* that took place in Central Park in New York City in 2010.

Going behind the scenes at your nonprofit

As someone who comes from the nonprofit sector, I can see the value of using a QR Code to share behind-the-scenes details that people would otherwise never see. This great opportunity allows you to cultivate existing supporters and recruit new ones.

Maybe your nonprofit delivers nutritious meals to the sick and homebound. By using a QR Code in your newsletter, brochure, or other marketing materials, you can link users to a video that shares the delivery of a wholesome meal and the driver's conversation with a person who may not have much other human contact. Head to Chapter 10 for other ways you can use QR Codes.

Chapter 8

Mitigating the Risks and Shortcomings of QR Codes

. . . .

In This Chapter

▶ Evaluating the danger that QR Codes pose to security and privacy

▶ Minimizing the risks of QR Codes

▶ Rebutting criticisms of QR Codes

. . . .

*T*here isn't a thing in this world that doesn't have some amount of risk, and QR Codes are no exception. Although QR Codes are great ways to link people to additional information you want to share about yourself and your business, they can be used in malicious ways.

In this chapter, I explain how cybercriminals are beginning to use QR Codes to manipulate people and steal their private information and money. Second, I show you how to protect yourself from these risks. Finally, I address how to rebut some of the common concerns over QR Codes so your plans to use them aren't stalled before you get started.

Eyeing the Risks That QR Codes Pose to Security and Privacy

The fact that QR Codes are so cheap and easy to make, and that consumers are so eager to scan them to see what they reveal, makes a QR Code a good tool for cybercriminals. Think about it: Scanning a QR Code poses a lot of the same threats as opening a dubious web page without any of the warnings that generally come with the latter.

One advantage of opening web pages is that you can see the link you're opening, and if it doesn't look right, you can pass on clicking it. That's not true with QR Codes. You just point and scan and don't really think about the risks.

The threat is that the QR Code could have a malicious URL embedded in it that takes you to site *malware* — short for *malicious software* — that can be, unbeknownst to you, installed on your mobile device. Malware can comprise your device's software and share sensitive information with cyber-criminals. Some of the ways that malware poses a threat to you include:

✔ **Making your calendar, contacts, and even credit card information available to criminals**

✔ **Stealing your Facebook, Google, and other passwords and posting without your knowledge or permission**

✔ **Tracking your location for criminal purposes**

✔ **Infecting your device with malware that can disable it**

The security and privacy threats QR Codes pose are real. Fortunately, documented cases of abuse are low, as QR Codes are just beginning to catch on with consumers. As interest in them grows, QR Codes could become a favorite for cybercriminals bent on exploiting unsuspecting users.

This all sounds dire, for sure, but you use your computer every day where the virus threat is probably a hundred-fold greater. It doesn't stop you from going online, nor should the risks of scanning QR Codes stop you either.

Why let the cybercriminals win!

The key is to do what you should do when faced with risks: Take precautions.

Taking Precautions

Try to take these precautions when scanning QR Codes:

- ✔ **Be careful of QR Code stickers.** Sometimes a cybercriminal will affix them over legitimate QR Codes.

- ✔ **Pay attention when you scan a QR Code.** There's an interim step between scanning the code and the launch of the browser, when you can see it's not going to be what you expected and you can abort the action. I bet you do this all the time online when you click a link and you just know it's headed to the wrong place. You might save yourself a lot of aggravation by keeping an eye on where you're headed.

- ✔ **Educate those who borrow your mobile device.** If you have kids that borrow you smartphone all the time, like my kids do, you should educate them on the potential hazards of QR Codes. This goes for anyone who might use your mobile device on a regular basis.

  Some QR Code readers let you see the URL on the code before it links you to the destination. Just remember that many QR Codes use shortened URLs so this strategy won't always work.

- ✔ **Be wary of QR Codes that say nothing about what they link to.** You learned earlier that a QR Code best practice is to the let people know what they get when they scan the QR Code.

Be especially careful if you have a mobile device that runs on the Android mobile operating system. Because Android is an open platform, cybercriminals can more easily exploit it. In search of articles on the risks of QR Codes to write this chapter, I was surprised that so many mentioned the vulnerability of Android devices. All the articles mentioned the importance of keeping your Android browser up to date and to scan only QR Codes from trusted sources.

Addressing Common Complaints about QR Codes

I have a saying when it comes to convincing people to try something: "Some will; some won't. So what? Next."

Some people are already riding the QR Code bandwagon, while others are convinced that QR Codes are sinister tools for an alien invasion and would never use them. Of course, most people are somewhere in between and aren't sure what to believe about QR Codes.

Here are the common complaints on QR Codes and how they can be addressed:

- ✓ **You have to download a QR Code reader.** Yes, QR Code readers aren't native to most mobile devices (although, as I point out in Chapter 2, many BlackBerry devices come with QR Code readers, which they call a barcode scanner). But you can easily download a free reader. Besides, most things you want for you mobile device don't come standard. The popular game Angry Birds has to be downloaded — and has been downloaded nearly 500 million times!

- ✓ **Only 6 percent of mobile users scan QR Codes.** Small? Yes. Insignificant? No. That still means 14 million people have scanned QR Codes! This number will grow as smartphone adoption increases (it's currently at 50%). Also, QR Codes are popular with young adults and a burgeoning tool for women and moms. If your product or service is geared toward one of these audiences, the percentage of your audience using QR Codes is much higher.

- ✓ **QR Codes are just clutter.** When they're not used well and don't enhance the user's experience, they are clutter. But when they're used well, these black-and-white portals to online content that can be as small as one square inch are great additions to the offline world.

- ✓ **QR Codes are boring.** They're boring only if you are. You can be as creative in QR Code design as you can in what you encode on them (see Figure 8-1). But remember, QR Codes are a tool to accomplish a goal and needn't be anything fancy. The QR Code itself isn't the Big Time; it's just the ticket to get in.

Figure 8-1: An animated QR Code courtesy of JESS3.

✔ **QR Code readers don't work.** Like anything, sometimes they don't. Sometimes it's not the reader but your connection to the Internet or a dated device. However, overall, QR Code readers are getting better and delivering faster scans with each new update.

✔ **Scanning a QR Code is a lot of work just to visit a website.** First, you should review Chapter 1 because QR Codes can do a lot more than just link you to a website. Second, I don't think it's easier to type a URL into my mobile browser when I could just scan a QR Code. Want to race? Finally, when done well, QR Codes can enhance a user's experience with content that goes deeper than those black-and-white squares let on. Try doing all that with a plain URL!

✔ **Why dedicate time and effort to QR Codes when they most likely will be replaced by something else?** QR Codes probably won't be around forever. The opportunity of QR Codes is similar to when brick-and-mortar businesses started selling online. The road was uncertain and clogged with glitches — but it was also wide open. Smart organizations that use QR Codes are embracing other new technologies, such as mobile, and are driving to a new customer experience. The road may seem lonely at times, but the destination is worth the trip.

Chapter 9

Embracing a Readable Future

Do you remember Atari, Google Wave and Buzz, and Friendster? What about Zip drives, Beta videos, MiniDiscs, or Pets.com with its dog sock puppet? Some of these may ring a bell because they all share something in common: They were all the latest and greatest technologies of their day. And now they don't exist anymore.

The current success of QR Codes stands in stark contrast to these failed ventures, but that's only because people are scanning these QR Codes with something besides a reader: their own rose-colored glasses.

No one knows what the future of QR Codes will be. In researching for this book, I came across article after article with headlines such as "QR Codes Are Dead" or profiles of a person or technology that would slay these apparently silly and ugly looking QR Codes. Still, I just bought a new color printer from one of the big office supply stores, and every sales tag in the electronics section had a QR Code on it!

The truth is that both sides are right. QR Codes are becoming more popular by the day, but ultimately they'll be replaced by something else.

In this chapter, I look at some of the alternatives to QR Codes that could one day replace the technology. I also explore what won't change: consumer appetite for everything mobile and a connection between the offline world and digital content.

Exploring Alternatives to QR Codes

Here are six alternatives to QR Codes that could either compete with code technology or replace it altogether.

Microsoft Tag

Of the six, Microsoft Tag (see Figure 9-1) is probably the most similar to QR Codes. Like QR Codes, Tag is a type of bar code that when scanned by a Tag reader links the user to online content.

Figure 9-1: Microsoft Tag.

Some of the advantages of Microsoft Tag include these:

- ✔ They're faster than QR Codes.
- ✔ You can store more data on a Tag than you can a QR Code.
- ✔ You can make them as small as ¾ inch. Generally, QR Codes should be one square inch or larger.

But Microsoft Tag has one big drawback: You can read them only with a Microsoft Tag reader, which may be acceptable if Microsoft mobile devices were as popular as iPhone, Android, and BlackBerry, but Microsoft devices command less than five percent of the market.

The chances are that Microsoft Tag will remain as niche as the parent company's mobile devices.

Google Goggles

Google Goggles is like regular Google search, but instead of inputting words to search, you open an app on your mobile device, take a picture, and search on the image.

For example, if I take a picture of Fenway Park (see Figure 9-2), where my hometown team the Boston Red Sox play, it brings up search results related to the park, its history, and how much the New York Yankees stink (at least it would if I were in charge of the results!).

Figure 9-2: Search results for Fenway Park using Google Goggles.

Google Goggles is interesting and useful, but the technology is new and it doesn't work on everything — yet. Also, in most instances, snapping a picture and searching on it takes you to search results, not a specific web page or destination.

For that reason alone, QR Codes are a better option.

Augmented reality

I must say that augmented reality is very, very cool. QR Codes connect the offline and online worlds, but augmented reality overlays the real world with digital content. *Augmented reality* is a live, direct or indirect, view of a physical, real-world environment whose elements are *augmented* by `computer-generated` sound, video, graphics or GPS data.

Consider this example: With augmented reality, you can let potential real estate buyers see the inside of a building from the sidewalk using their smartphones. They just align the screen of their phone with the building, as if they were taking a picture or recording video, and digital data overlays the image, showing what's inside.

This informational video from Layar (scan the QR Code in Figure 9-3), a company pioneering this technology, shows some of the incredible uses of augmented reality.

Figure 9-3: Scan this QR Code with a reader to see augmented reality in action.

This is interesting technology, but it won't be mainstream for at least a few years. QR Codes will be the workhorse that fills this gap until the technology and devices needed to run it become, well, a reality.

Near field communication

Near field communication (or NFC) involves a mobile device and an NFC chip. When the device is placed close to the chip, which can be placed in many things (see Figure 9-4), including another phone, it prompts the device to take a specific action (such as open a web page, dial a phone number, share a picture or video, and so on).

Figure 9-4: NFC is a great option for mobile payments.

NFC between two devices works similar to the Bump app you might have used on your smartphone to exchange contact information. Although Bump uses different technology, the swap is initiated by two enabled devices "bumping" together for a just a second or two.

NFC is very easy to use. Just put your smartphone near an NFC chip and you're done. No scanning, no reader, no holding up your phone. You don't even need to physically "bump" the devices.

One of the challenges of NFC, however, is that an NFC chip can't be put in a magazine ad, business card, or anything else printed. Using a QR Code is much easier.

I could see a happy coexistence between QR Codes and NFC because the latter is so easy to use, but can't be used everywhere like a QR Code can.

Accepting What Won't Change

No one really knows what will become of QR Codes in the long run, but we can be fairly certain of a few things that will drive QR Code use and development.

- ✓ **The mobile screen will be the most dominant screen in history.** Just as I began to write this section today, a study done by Chitika showed that web traffic for Apple's mobile operating system, called iOS, surpassed web traffic on Apple's laptop and desktop operating system, OS X. People prefer to use their mobile devices for just about everything.

- ✓ **Just about everyone will own a phone.** Mobile phone sales are expected to hit a billion units in 2015. That means one out of every seven people on the planet will own a smartphone. Just last year, 250 million Android phones sold, or eight phones per second!

- ✓ **Other devices are evolving into smartphones.** Take cameras, which have boasted their own array of technological improvements during the past few years. The camera that comes on many mobile devices is so darn convenient that camera makers have responded with cameras that look and act more like smartphones.

- ✓ **Wi-Fi is coming to your area soon.** The Wireless Broadband Alliance reported in 2011 that global public Wi-Fi hotspot numbers are set to grow from 1.3 million in 2011 to 5.8 million by 2015, a 350 percent increase. The Alliance also found that smartphones are poised to surpass laptops as the device most frequently connected to Wi-Fi. QR Codes need a reliable Internet connection, and the Wi-Fi industry is stepping up to meet the challenge.

- ✓ **Consumers are addicted to their smartphones.** I know how I am when I forget my phone at home. I feel disconnected and tense, and I bet you do too. Smartphone users spend nearly 90 minutes per day just using apps on their devices and 75 minutes surfing the web. That's nearly three hours per day of mobile device use. But consider this: The average adult spends more than seven hours per day consuming media. Mobile use could double in the years ahead. It's no surprise that when asked to choose between only their smartphone or desktop for six months, 55 percent of respondents under 30 chose their phones.

✓ **Consumers are warming up to mobile purchases.** One in two mobile users uses their mobile device in stores to make purchasing decisions. They're also buying items on their phone, totaling $9 billion in purchases in 2011.

✓ **Mobile devices will be the remote control of people's lives.** A recent Nielsen study showed that people use smartphones for everything: music, news, dining, games, weather, directions, banking, and more. Heck, 40 percent of people use their mobile device while watching television. And the television industry is taking note, with innovations that link viewers to their favorite shows and will one day allow them to buy the things they see by just pointing their phones at their televisions and clicking a button. People want that connection between the offline and online worlds. QR Codes are the bridge.

Mobile devices are everywhere. Connectivity to the Internet is growing worldwide. Mobile devices rank pretty close to food, water, and shelter as a thing people think they need to live. People want a remote control for their lives (see Figure 9-5).

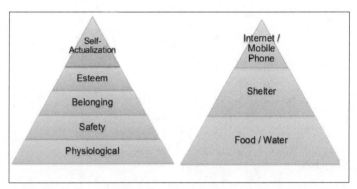

Figure 9-5: Maslow's hierarchy of needs revisited for the mobile age.

The future of QR Codes may seem like the maze people often mistake them for. It's a maze that may lead to something better, or to something else. Or it may just lead to a dead end.

But the path of mobile use is straight and clear. People may not scan QR Codes forever, but demand for online content to enhance and support offline activities is strong. For now, QR Codes are the best way to link the two.

Chapter 10

Ten Practical Uses for QR Codes

. . . .

In This Chapter

▶ Exploring different ways to use QR Codes

▶ Using QR Codes to save trees, to put more money in your pocket, and to preserve your memory for generations to come.

. . . .

*T*his book shares a lot about QR Codes, including how to read them, how to make them, and how to measure their effectiveness, among other things. This chapter is all about how to *use* them creatively and effectively to accomplish what all good marketing should do: to woo new customers and to keep your current ones coming back.

Showing the Behind-the-Scenes Process

If you run a company or nonprofit and find yourself always saying, "If only people could see how we do things!," QR Codes are the tool for you. QR Codes aren't just a bridge from the offline world to digital content. They can be a looking glass into a world that people probably never see — but should.

Say that you run a restaurant and you have a number of specialty items that take a good deal of time and care to prepare. This process is largely lost to the diner, who just sees a menu item and price. But by including a QR Code next to specific items on the menu, the diner can see right from her seat the chef's early morning trip to the docks to pick the best fish, how carefully the fish is deboned and prepared for cooking, and how sparklingly clean the kitchen is.

These types of things deepen a diner's appreciation for the meal and, perhaps, the steep price they may be paying for it.

 Another place where details and process are appreciated is the premium beer industry, where customers are discerning and enjoy learning about the beer they're drinking. Microbrewery WJ King owns the bragging rights as the first brewery in the world to put their head brewer into every pub. The brewery has added a unique QR Code to the pump clip and bottle label of each of its 25 beers. When you scan the QR in the left margin, you're linked to a video featuring head brewer Ian Burgess talking about that specific beer and the ingredients from which it's made.

Delivering Real-Time Information

QR Codes are a great way to share breaking information about everything from the latest local news to changes in the bus schedule. A smart example of the latter is the Metro West Yorkshire in England using QR Codes to deliver the latest news on everything from the next bus arrival to route changes to closures due to weather or special events.

The QR Codes are displayed at 45 bus stops and serve another important function, according to Metro Chairman Councillor James Lewis. By scanning the codes, riders can get a permanent bus schedule right on their phones.

I'd love to see QR Codes on sport tickets. You could scan the QR Code on your ticket the day of the event for the latest information on weather delays, special attractions, discounts on team apparel, suggestions for getting to the event, and best places to park.

Getting Customer Feedback

QR Codes are a great way to gather timely customer feedback. Instead of having customers fill out a paper form and assigning an employee to enter the information into a computer database — or asking customers to fill out a survey on their home computer — you can use a QR Code.

To get feedback from diners, my local Italian restaurant includes a QR Code on the receipt that links to a mobile page where diners can enter a personalized code (see Figure 10-1a).

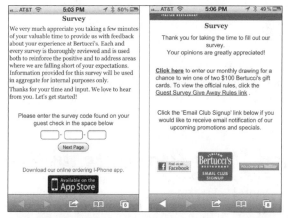

Figure 10-1: Scanning the QR Code takes you to a mobile page where you can review your dining experience. (a) One QR Code links the diner to the survey, then a contest, and finally to social media sites. (b)

After completing the survey, you're encouraged to enter a monthly drawing for a $100 gift card. This is smart because now the restaurant is trying to capture your e-mail address as well. I also like the fact that they give you the chance to link to their Facebook and Twitter accounts (see Figure 10-1b).

Another industry where QR Codes are needed for prompt customer feedback is healthcare. Hospitals can use QR Codes to get feedback from patients, instead of distributing the hard copy surveys that sometimes take weeks to get back.

A group of healthcare administration graduate students at Penn State University envision placards in waiting rooms and inpatient and outpatient areas that ask patients and their families a simple but important question: "How are we treating you today?"

People can walk up to the placard, use the QR Code applications on their phones to scan the appropriate area — green for good, red for bad — and be directed to a response-specific web survey to share their concerns and comments. Ideally, a patient response team would respond immediately to the concerns. Hospitals would have a patient-experience response team on call 24/7 to deal with concerns immediately.

Restaurants and hospitals are just two kinds of businesses that could benefit from the timely, fast customer feedback that QR Codes can deliver. Additionally, building managers can post QR Codes, so tenants can alert the janitor to an issue. Local parks can use QR Codes so visitors can comment on a new playground or report an overflowing garbage can or vandalism.

Selling Your Products or Services

In Chapter 7, I talk about how retailers are using a service called `Give.mobi` and QR Codes to encourage consumers to support their favorite nonprofits. The QR Code links users to a mobile-ready page where they can make a donation via PayPal or enter their credit card information. You can use the same process to sell your products and services.

A sign of things to come here in the United States is a trial program by PayPal in Singapore that allows commuters in 15 metro stations to make purchases using QR Codes (see Figure 10-2). It takes only three easy steps. Commuters scan the QR Code next to the product they want to purchase, pay via PayPal or credit card, and choose either pickup or delivery. That's it!

Buying stuff with QR Codes is easy when you have an account with PayPal (or with Google Wallet, or with a host of other competitors that hope to make a fortune in this profitable space) because you don't have to keep reentering your credit card information.

Figure 10-2: Shopping off a wall.

Initiating a program like this in Singapore makes sense because smartphone adoption is 70 percent, nearly twenty points higher than in the United States. However, with the rise of mobile devices in the U.S., it's only a matter of time before the much-touted *mobile wallet* becomes a reality here.

LevelUp, a Boston based startup, is using QR Codes to make mobile payments more mainstream with small businesses. If you've ever used Starbucks mobile payment app or stood in line behind someone who did, LevelUp works much in the same way. After you sign up and register a credit card number with LevelUp, you get a unique QR Code that can either be scanned by a smartphone or waved in front of a terminal at the business. After Starbucks, LevelUp (www.thelevelup.com) is the second largest player in the mobile payment sector, processing nearly a million dollar in payments a month.

Generating Leads

If you're looking to generate more sales leads for your company, try using QR Codes in a practical but creative way.

- ✓ **Business cards:** But just don't link to your boring contact info. They have that on your card. Instead, link the QR Code to a customer testimonial on your outstanding products or service.

- ✓ **PowerPoint slides:** Instead of linking the code to your website or phone number, link to content (such as an article, post, or video) that gives more in-depth information about your topic from a third-party source. Show them it's about them, not you.

✓ **"For Sale" signs:** If you're selling your home, don't just link the QR Code to the information sheet — shoot a video giving people a tour of your home and end it with, "If you liked what you saw on the first floor, the second floor is even better. Open house this Sunday."

✓ **Restaurant tables:** Have half go to Facebook where diners can like your page, and the other half go to Foursquare, the location-based service that allows you to share your location to friends and followers.

✓ **Tradeshow booths:** Include them on your booth and materials and have your team show attendees how to scan and save them for later (when they'll have time to look at your information).

✓ **Waiting areas:** Put QR Codes in elevators, ski lifts, check-out lines, and even bathrooms! (Don't laugh. Thirty-nine percent of smartphone users have admitted to using their phones in the potty.)

✓ **Print ads and posters:** Give consumers directions to your business and info on what time you open and close.

✓ **Reordering:** Include QR Codes on packaging and invoices that takes shoppers to where they can reorder with just a couple of clicks.

✓ **Polls:** Ask your customers to take a quick poll on where they heard about your business or what they liked about shopping with you.

✓ **Appointments:** Use a QR Code to link prospects directly with your calendar. I use an online calendar service called `Tungle.com` that allows others to see my availability but not my appointments. Visitors can pick a date and time to speak or meet with me. To see how this works, scan the QR Code in the left margin to visit my Tungle calendar.

✓ **Testing:** Put QR Codes on all your advertising so you can track scans and identify tech-savvy audiences.

✓ **Tattoos:** Kids love the temporary ones. Why give away a QR Code tattoo that links to coloring pages or a funny video with your logo.

- ✔ **Products:** No salesperson around? No problem. QR Codes can give shoppers all the specs and details they need.

- ✔ **Coupons:** Consumers love coupons. Reward their scans with savings.

- ✔ **E-mail newsletter:** Shoppers can sign up for yours by scanning a QR Code and entering an e-mail address.

- ✔ **Store windows:** Show people what's inside or give them some details on the displayed items.

- ✔ **When you're closed:** You can tell people when you'll reopen or give them a video tour of your showroom.

Making an Impression

QR Codes currently enjoy an enviable place in society. They have a "What's that?" quality that will be short lived but should be used for all it's worth while it lasts.

I had a similar experience when I bought Apple's iPad shortly after it arrived on the market in spring 2010. I used to bring it with me to my local coffee shop, and people would stand behind me to check it out and ask me questions. I was the cool guy with new tech tool! Now when I bring my iPad to that same coffee shop, no one stops to stare because they're too busy looking at their own iPad.

For a short time, QR Codes will be the tech tool people point to and whisper about. The question is, how can you benefit from the coolness factor that comes with them? Check out these ways:

- ✔ **Enhance your resume.** If you're a graphic designer on the job hunt, include a stylish QR Code on your resume or portfolio that will catch an employer's eye.

  You can see some examples of cool QR Codes on my Pinterest board "QR Codes For Dummies." Just scan the QR Code in the left margin.

- ✔ **Highlight your knowledge of QR Codes.** If your sights are set on a job in marketing or social media, consider including a QR Code on your resume, business card, cover letter, and the like. Not only can the QR Code link to valuable additional information about your professional qualifications, QR Codes are a great talking point. It's one of those things that are bound to bring up questions. The key is to make sure that your explanation of what QR Codes are, what they do, and how they can be used is as smooth and easy as scanning a QR Code with a reader.

✔ **Incorporate codes in your business.** Suggest to your boss a way that you can use QR Codes in a simple and effective way in your business. Maybe it's something as easy as putting them on purchase receipts so shoppers can quickly scan a QR Code and talk to a customer service representative if they have a problem.

✔ **Spice up your next event with QR Codes.** Include them on your invitation to get people's attention while sharing important details, such as directions to the event location or a fun recap video of last year's event.

An easy way to make an impression with QR Codes is to forget the traditional black-and-white design and customize yours with color, artwork, or your logo. See Chapter 3 for details.

Going Paperless

One of the things I like about technology is that it reduces our paper use. I hate when trees end up in trash barrels as paper waste, or even recycling. The key is to stop using paper. I pride myself on how long I can go between printing and copying something. QR Codes have helped me set a personal record!

Save paper and space by printing your QR Codes on mailing labels instead of wasting a whole sheet of paper by trying one of these ideas:

✔ **Post your itinerary.** If I'm taking a trip, I'll post a QR Code on our kitchen bulletin board that links to a document with my itinerary on it. If my itinerary changes, I just update the document, and the QR Codes always link to the most recently updated version.

✔ **Share recipes and notes.** If you're a baker like my wife is, you can link a QR Code to your notes on a specific recipe, or a picture of the finished product. This is especially useful when people ask you for a recipe. You can give them the recipe, and your tips for making it, on a QR Code.

✔ **Link to your online newsletter.** Forget printed newspapers and newsletters — put QR Codes in prominent places where readers can scan them for their weekly mobile edition.

✔ **Distribute supplementary materials.** If you're a teacher, save some paper and use a QR Code to share class notes, handouts, or the entire lecture on a podcast.

✔ **Save on mailing costs.** Why are you still mailing out a 300-page catalog when you can send a postcard with a QR Code on it that links to a full-color online catalog?

✔ **Streamline your work flow.** With QR Codes, manufacturers can implement a point-and-browse experience on the shop floor. If work orders listing collections of parts included a QR Code, a technician with a mobile device can scan the work order and immediately pull up the latest approved assembly procedure.

✔ **Sell your house.** Stop printing out reams of paper for that open house your agent is hosting this weekend -and give her a QR Code that potential home buyers can scan. Find out who's really interested, and who isn't.

Replacing SMS Text with QR Codes

If you haven't done an SMS text campaign before, I bet you've seen one, perhaps at a store or in an ad you've seen. An advertisement might say something like this: "Get exclusive monthly discounts; text SHOP to 55555." (In the example, *SHOP* is called the *keyword,* and the five-digit number is called the *short code.*)

When a user does this, he's added to a database from which you can send him future text messages.

SMS text is popular with marketers, but QR Codes may be a better alternative. Here are some advantages that the QR Codes have over SMS text campaigns:

✔ Scanning a QR Code is easier than sending a text. QR Codes involve no typing, just button pressing and scanning.

✔ QR Codes can directly link to rich media, whereas SMS text gives you a link that you have to click to access content.

✔ QR Codes have a newness factor that SMS text doesn't. It's new, easy, and cool — just the things consumers like.

✔ QR Codes are visual and more attractive and enticing to consumers than a keyword and short code. QR Codes can also be customized with color or artwork.

✔ QR Codes can link to just about anything, not just a URL.

✔ QR codes can store more than 4,000 alphanumeric characters.

✔ Using a QR Code means no text charges from your telephone carrier.

Still, marketers need to consider their audience before swapping QR Codes for SMS text. Consumers are still warming up to QR Codes, and not everyone owns the smartphone needed to scan them.

Your best bet may be to include both SMS text and QR Codes in your next campaign and measure the response to each one before choosing which is right for you (see Figure 10-3).

Figure 10-3: Combine SMS with QR Codes.

Delivering Customer Service

A great benefit of QR Codes is that they can be a virtual link between your company and your customers. They can be there when you're not to answer questions, to give information, or to say thank you.

- If you run a hotel or recreation area, you can use QR Codes to answer popular questions about where to eat, what to do, or where to shop.

- If you own a fitness center, put QR Codes on machines and equipment that link to a brief video on how to use them safely and effectively.

- If you run a business that's known for its long lines, use QR Codes to share wait time or entertainment to keep people happy.

- Snap pictures of customers enjoying themselves at attractions or on rides and give them a QR Code that takes them to a web page where they can find their picture in a frame with your business name on it.

- If you sell cars, put QR Codes in areas where drivers can learn how to perform basic maintenance on their cars. For example, include one that links drivers to a video on how to properly change a tire.

- If you sell lawn and yard equipment, put QR Codes on them that link to manuals or a web page where people can make a service appointment.

Preserving Your Memory

If after reading this book, you've truly fallen in love with QR Codes, I have good news for you: You can take them with you.

You see, the growth of QR Codes in the tombstone business is anything but dead. Headstone companies are giving their customers an afterlife with QR Codes on tombstones that link to everything from pictures to videos to audio messages from the recently deceased (see Figure 10-4). Kind of creepy, huh?

Figure 10-4: Headstone with QR Code.

For a small fee, companies such as Seattle-based Living Headstones will affix a QR Code to a new or existing headstone and link it to a personalized web page . . . forever. You can even password-protect it so that only families and friends can access it.

Of course, thanks to this book, you can make your own QR Code and link it to anything you want. Just make sure you put it on something durable so that it will withstand the elements and the test of time.

Lastly, remember that like most things, QR Codes won't be around forever. They'll eventually be replaced by something else. You can prepare for the inevitable by using QR Codes that can be easily removed and replaced on headstones with new technology as times change. The only thing that should be a permanent part of a headstone is what's under it!

Index